50 WAYS TO IMPROVE YOUR WEATHER FORECASTING

Published by Adlard Coles Nautical
an imprint of A & C Black Publishers Ltd
38 Soho Square, London W1D 3HB
www.adlardcoles.com

ISBN 978-0-7136-8268-7

A CIP catalogue record for this book is available from the British Library.

A & C Black uses paper produced with elemental chlorine-free pulp, harvested from managed sustainable forests.

Printed and bound in Spain

Note: While all reasonable care has been taken in the publication of this book, the publisher takes no responsibility for the use of the methods or products described in the book.

ACKNOWLEDGEMENTS

I would like to thank the following for assistance with photos, drawings and help:

UK Met Office
NOAA
Maxsea
Smartcom
Cmap

Thanks also to all those who have had faith in my weather forecasting over the years on such epic challenges as the Virgin Atlantic Challenger Atlantic record attempts, the Azimut Atlantic Challenger Atlantic record attempt, the Destriero Atlantic record attempt, plus various Round Britain and London-Monte Carlo record attempts. As a forecaster, you tend to be remembered for the ones you get wrong, not the ones you get right.

WAYS TO IMPROVE YOUR WEATHER FORECASTING

DAG PIKE

ADLARD COLES NAUTICAL
LONDON

contents

50 WAYS TO IMPROVE YOUR WEATHER FORECASTING

WEATHER FORECASTS

INTERPRETING THE FORECASTS

FINE-TUNING THE FORECAST

THE WIND AND THE SEA

contents

LOCAL WEATHER CONDITIONS

TACTICS AND SHORT-TERM CHANGES

1 WHEN TO GO TO SEA

GET THE BEST POSSIBLE WEATHER INFORMATION BEFORE YOU LEAVE HARBOUR.

The weather dictates much of what can be done at sea, so you need the best information about the weather that is available if you want to go to sea without nasty surprises. While forecasts can tell a major part of the weather story, they need your input if they are going to be used successfully. The weather forecast will be your basic guide, but making the decision about when to go to sea and what tactics to employ is something that you, not the weather forecaster, must do. Many people blame the forecaster when things don't turn out as planned, but in the majority of cases it is the yachtsman or motorboater involved who should take responsibility.

To start with, the forecast will give a general picture of what weather conditions you can expect, but it doesn't usually indicate what the sea conditions will be like. It is the sea conditions rather than the wind that can have an important bearing on both comfort and safety at sea, and these conditions will really be your main concern when you are leaving port. Most sailors will have a general idea of the sea conditions that can be expected in various wind conditions but sea conditions can also be greatly affected by local topography, shallow water and tides – you need to interpret the forecast bearing these factors in mind.

Even the wind strengths given in forecasts can often span a considerable range of conditions. The forecaster may predict wind strengths of between, say, force 5 and force 7; here, you are presented with conditions that at the top end of the forecast range may be too strong for you yet at the bottom end could be just right for a fine day's sailing.

So when you get the forecast before going to sea, stop and think about it quite carefully. Study it in relation to the sea areas you will be sailing in and make your own assessment of what conditions will be like, both at the time of sailing and during the course of your passage. If you are in any doubt about whether conditions will be suitable, go out and have a look to see what it is really like out there. Do this knowing that you have the option of turning round and coming back if you don't like what you see. Also look for stopping places along the route where the day's sailing could be abandoned if the conditions turn out to be worse than expected. Keep your options open as much as you can but remember it is you, not the forecaster, who has to make the final decision about whether conditions are suitable for you, your crew and your boat.

MAKING THE DECISION ABOUT WHEN TO GO TO SEA IS SOMETHING THAT YOU, NOT THE WEATHER FORECASTER, MUST DO.

2 NEGOTIATING WITH THE WEATHER

We tend to think of the weather as something absolute, something that is cast in stone and can't be changed. Well, yes, you cannot actually change the weather, but remember that it is constantly changing and will also change considerably with time. The forecast can reveal a good part of what is happening and what is going to happen, but the factors you can determine will allow you to have a degree of control and let you negotiate with the weather.

Although you can't change the weather, your power of negotiation lies in your ability to decide where you are and where you are going to be in relation to the changing weather patterns. By using the factor of time, you can exercise considerable control over the weather you experience, because the weather will be changing as time progresses. By using the element of time in this way, you may decide to delay your departure for a day or so; but even delaying departure by an hour or two can allow a front to pass through your position. The passage of a front in this way can produce a significant change in the weather you experience when you set off.

In order to negotiate with the weather, you will need the best possible weather information you can obtain, and this

COLD FRONT CHARACTERISTICS

ELEMENT	IN ADVANCE OF THE FRONT	AT THE FRONT	BEHIND THE FRONT
Pressure	Falls	Sudden rise	Slow continuous rise
Wind	Backs and increases	Veers suddenly often with line squalls and severe winds	Slowly backing after squalls then steady
Temperature	Steady but sometimes a slight fall in rain	Sudden fall	Little change
Cloud	Altocumulus and Altostratus followed by Cumulonimbus	Cumulonimbus with Fractostratus or low Nimbostratus	Lifts rapidly but Cumulus or Cumulonimbus may develop
Weather	Some rain with possible thunder	Heavy rain possibly with hail and thunder	Heavy rain then fine periods and showers
Visibility	Poor with some fog	Temporary deterioration then rapid improvement	Very good

should relate to your individual location as far as possible. Of particular importance is the timing of any weather changes that are forecast to occur. You will need to relate these to your current position, and local observations such as rain density and clouds can often provide you with an indication of impending change. The more information you have and the better the quality of that information, the stronger will be your negotiating position in regard to the weather. The difference in the quality of the information you obtain could mean a day spent at sea rather than holed up in harbour.

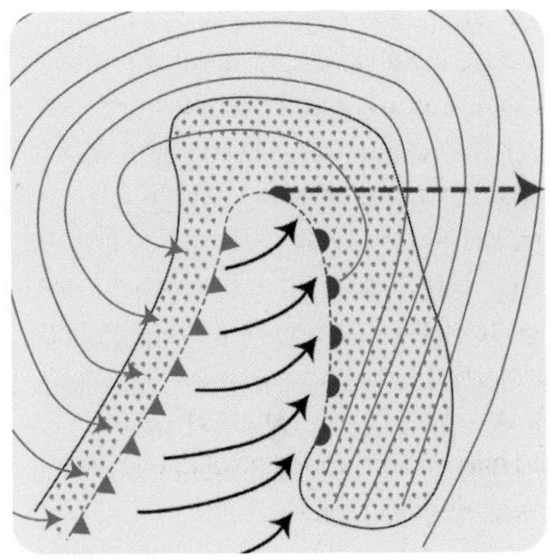

A TYPICAL NORTHERN HEMISPHERE DEPRESSION WITH THE SHADED SECTION SHOWING THE MAIN AREAS AND THE BROKEN ARROW SHOWING THE DIRECTION OF TRAVEL. THE STRONGER ARROWS DENOTE THE WARM AIR SECTION OF THE DEPRESSION.

WARM FRONT CHARACTERISTICS

ELEMENT	IN ADVANCE OF THE FRONT	AT THE FRONT	BEHIND THE FRONT
Pressure	Steady falls	Fall ceases	Little change
Wind	Backs and increases	Veers and decreases	Steady
Temperature	Steady or slow rise	Rises slowly	Little change
Cloud	Ci, Cs, As, Ns in succession	Low Nimbostratus and Fractostratus	Stratus and Stratocumulus
Weather	Continuous rain or snow	Precipitation almost stops	Fair or intermittent slight rain or drizzle
Visibility	Good except in the snow	Poor with mist and low cloud	Often poor with low cloud and mist or fog

3 WEATHER IN THE FOURTH DIMENSION

We saw in Negotiating with the weather, 2, how time can be important in weather forecasting. We are used to weather being presented to us in two dimensions, as is the case with the weather patterns shown on a weather map. For marine use, this two-dimensional weather is adequate for a snapshot of likely conditions, but there is also a vertical component to the weather. This will be of more interest to fliers than boaters, but we can see the evidence of this in the way the weather behaves in a front or in a squall or a thunderstorm. For the sailor, it is the fourth dimension of the weather – the factor of time – that can be vitally important when working out what's to come and when.

Weather forecasts tend to cover fixed periods of time, usually 12 or 24 hour periods, and each forecast can cover a considerable area. While you will obviously be interested in the general weather patterns, what you really need to know is what the weather conditions will be like along the route you are planning to take and in the locations you will reach at a particular time. Unless you get a personalised forecast, it is up to you to interpret the general forecast and tailor it to your specific requirements - which involves considering the factor of time.

The best basic tool for this is to obtain two or more consecutive weather charts. By comparing these, you can get a good idea of how the weather patterns are changing over time. These consecutive weather charts will show the movement of the weather fronts and the wind changes associated with them, so that you can estimate much more accurately when changes will occur in your particular locality.

You can do this with traditional paper forecast charts, but a better solution, using modern technology, is to study computer programs that show moving weather patterns. Computer-generated weather charts are still based mainly on weather information that is processed every 12 hours, but with computer technology all the weather patterns during these 12 hour periods can be shown with the changes every hour or so. By using these sequential weather charts, you can obtain a much better picture of the changing weather patterns and get a real handle on the fourth dimension of the weather. These moving charts allow you to see how the changes relate to your current and proposed positions.

WEATHER IN THE FOURTH DIMENSION

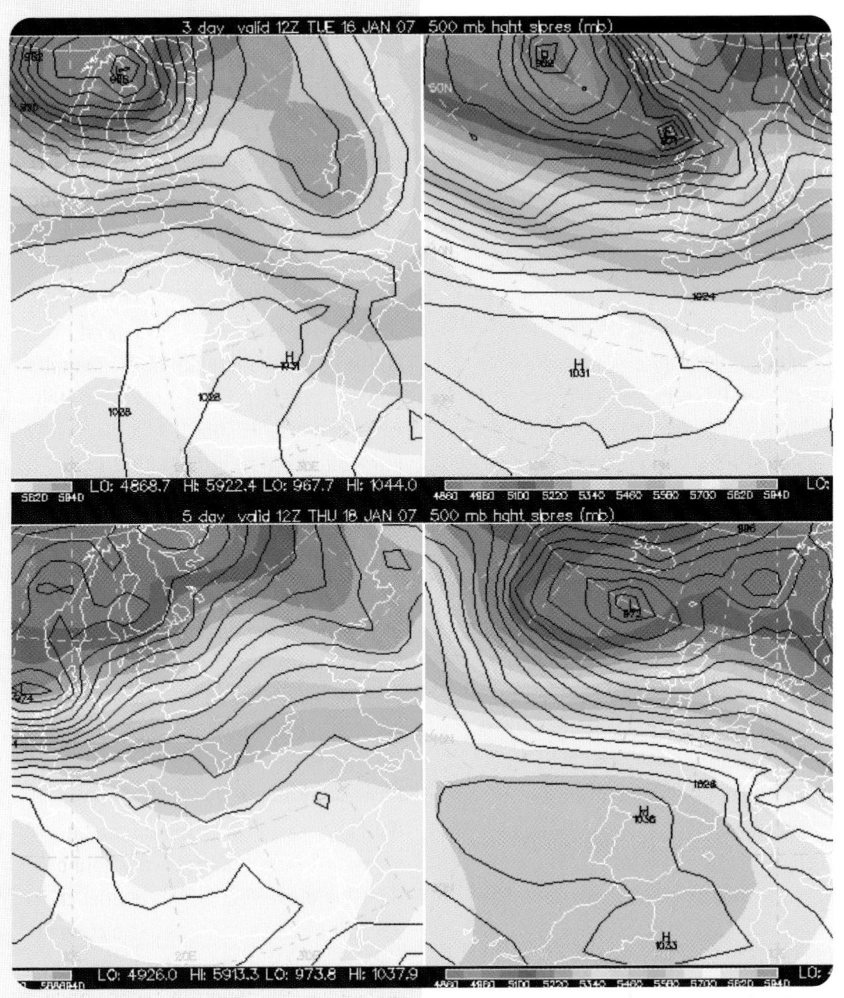

FOUR CONSECUTIVE FORECASTS THAT CAN HELP YOU GET A PICTURE OF THE WEATHER IN FOUR DIMENSIONS.

4 THE LIMITATIONS OF FORECASTS

There are two main types of weather forecast used by the sailor – the weather map and the written or verbal type of forecast. In understanding and using these forecasts, it is important to recognise their limitations, how much you can rely on them and just what they mean.

These days, computer software predicts the future weather patterns based largely on historical similarities. It is the computer that generates the weather maps, which are then checked and possibly fine-tuned using the skills of experienced weather forecasters.

Most of the time the predictions generated by the computer are accurate and the system is tried and tested to a high level of accuracy. The problems arise when there are local anomalies in the weather that the computer software may not detect, and when the smooth contours of the isobars on the forecast chart hide local changes and differences. Forecasters are likely to err on the side of caution in developing the verbal or written forecast from the forecast charts, which means they are likely to offer a worse-case scenario, forecasting conditions that could actually exist but may not be the general pattern. Their forecasts won't take into account any local conditions that may affect the weather.

All of this means that the forecasts are likely to have limitations on their reliability and accuracy as far as specific requirements are concerned. To get the best out of a forecast, you need to add your input into the equation and interpret the data for your own particular requirements. This personal input is an essential feature in counteracting the limitations of the general forecast to give you a better understanding of the weather you can expect.

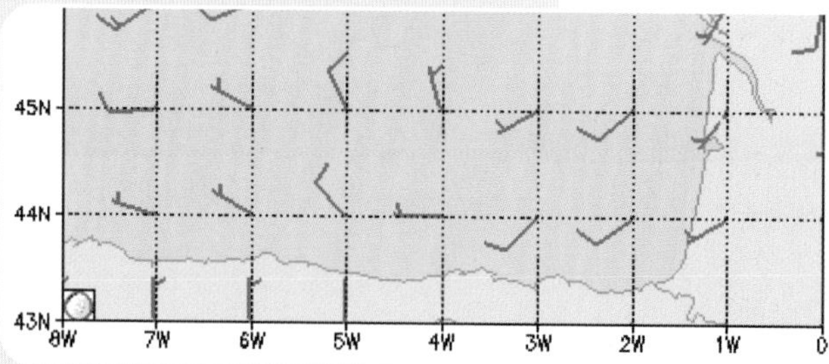

FORECAST WINDS FOR SEA AREA BISCAY, SHOWING THE WIDE RANGE OF WIND STRENGTHS AND DIRECTION.

QUESTIONING THE FORECASTS

5

The weather forecast generally sounds very definite and you may feel that you cannot question it. This is particularly the case with radio and TV forecasts and those issued over the Navtex system, where you tend to focus on your particular area rather than gaining a more general weather picture. However, you would do well to question the accuracy of the forecast if you want to obtain the most reliable information.

You can often get an indication of a forecast's reliability by looking at how many variable factors are included. When the forecast says 'winds force 4 to 5, perhaps force 6', this should suggest that the forecaster is not entirely sure what's going to happen. The difference in wind strength from lowest to highest could mean almost double the wind strength over the forecaster's given range.

This apparent vagueness can make it very difficult to decide on a course of action. However, you can get a clearer picture if you study carefully the options being offered. Remember that the forecaster will often be hampered in giving a precise forecast because the forecast has to cover a large area of sea. Weather can change considerably over 500-650km (300-400 miles) of sea area but the forecaster has to cater for all parts of the region in one compact forecast.

You can help to clarify matters by knowing your position within the sea area and having a better understanding of what is going on. If you know that the weather patterns are moving from west to east and you are in the western part of the sea area, then you will experience any forecast changes early on. Weather maps can be of great assistance, as you can see how the weather is developing and moving; and local signs and conditions, which we will discuss later, can also remove some of the questions.

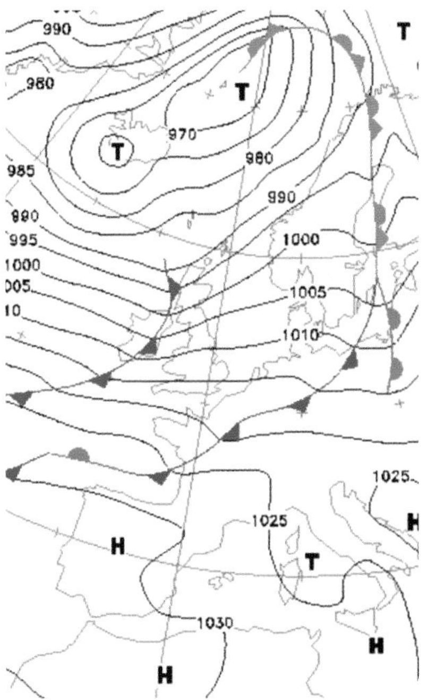

THE SORT OF DETAILED WEATHER MAP THAT CAN HELP YOU TO BOTH UNDERSTAND AND QUESTION THE FORECAST IN YOUR AREA.

6 EVOLVING WEATHER

Weather conditions are rarely static; they are a constantly moving and changing pattern of events. By being able to get a picture of these changing events, you can have a much better 'feel' for the weather and get a clearer idea of what is going to happen. Obviously the weather forecasts will give you a pretty good indication of the imminent changes that are likely to occur, and even some of the longer-term developing patterns of the weather. However, having an understanding of the way in which the weather is evolving and developing will be a great help in gaining that all-important feel for the weather.

Weather charts are the best way to obtain this evolving picture, because from these you can see how the high- and low-pressure areas and the various fronts are moving and interacting. A succession of charts at the normal 12 hour intervals should enable you to see how the general weather patterns are developing and changing. You will also be able to see how low-pressure systems and their associated fronts, which tend to bring most of the bad weather and changes in the weather, are moving. Perhaps most importantly, you will be able to get an impression of the speed at which the various systems are moving and this should enable you to put a more accurate timing on changes that are forecast to occur. This timing information can be vital for planning your weather strategy.

When you are planning to head out to sea, you will tend to focus on obtaining weather charts showing the future movements of the weather patterns. These are obviously important to show what is going to happen, but you can get a much better feel for the evolving weather patterns if you also look at the historical changes to give an indication of what has been going on for the past day or two. This will help a great deal to put the current weather situation into perspective.

It can be surprisingly difficult to get hold of historical weather charts. It seems that once the weather has happened, the charts are quickly discarded. This means that when you're planning to go to sea you should start looking at the weather charts a day or two beforehand. In this way, you will already have that all-important 'feel' for the weather and the flow of weather patterns, and this will enable you to understand what is going to happen in the future.

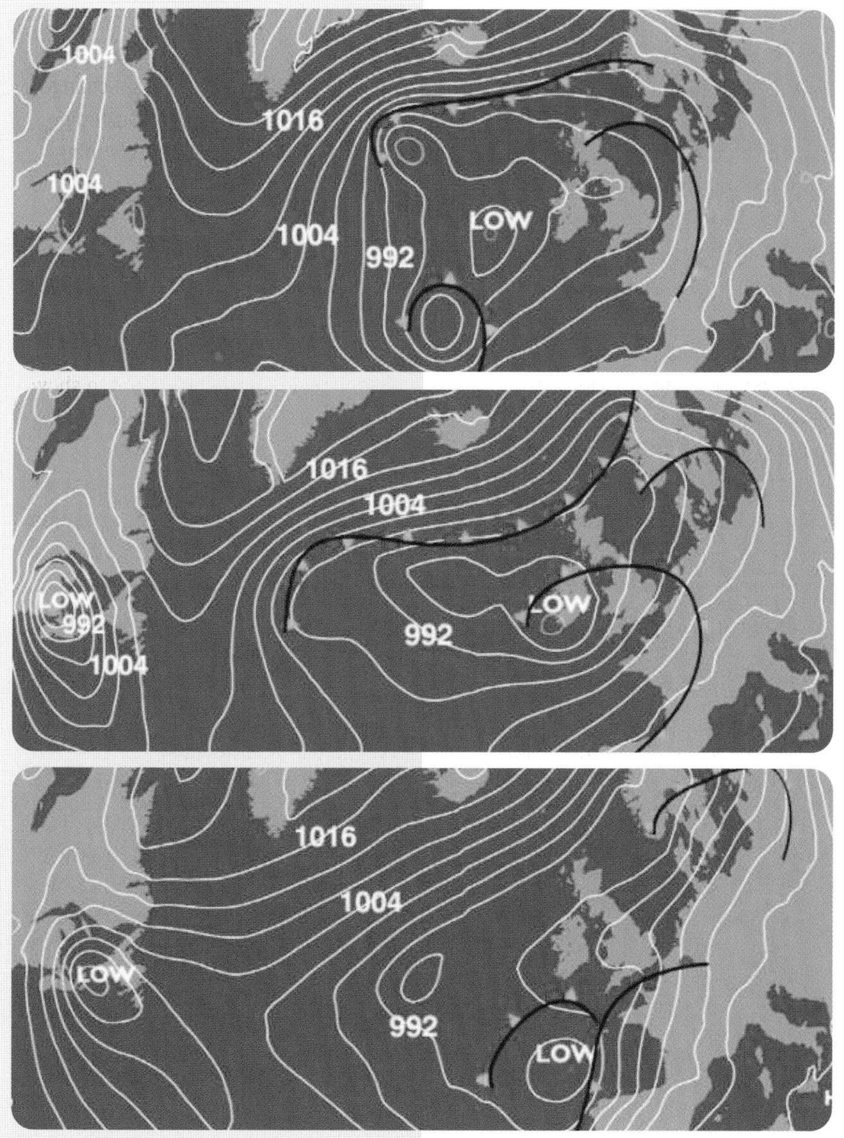

THREE CONSECUTIVE FORECAST MAPS THAT CAN HELP YOU TO UNDERSTAND EVOLVING WEATHER PATTERNS.

7 YOU GET WHAT YOU PAY FOR

There is a huge amount of weather information available from different sources and it is important to be aware of the quality of the information you are getting. You get what you pay for with weather forecasts – therefore, the more you pay, the more accurate and personal your weather information is likely to be. The weather forecasts on radio and television are free and tend to give you a broad outline of the weather and what changes to expect. The accuracy is generally good but sometimes rather vague, particularly in terms of timing. It can also be quite general because of the large areas that the forecast may cover, and forecasters will often present a worst-case scenario rather than the accurate detail that you require for planning your strategy.

Navtex is also free (once you have paid for the receiver), but the quality of the information is not likely to be any higher than that found on radio and TV. The Internet is a vast reservoir of weather information and here you can get 5 day weather charts for free, plus satellite pictures, but again the forecasts tend to be general.

If you have the weather maps, you can do your own interpretation of these and come up with a reasonably good forecast once you have honed your forecasting skills. You have to remember that these Internet weather charts will generally be at least 12 hours apart, so you will have to interpolate between the charts to get a more accurate picture of the timing of events.

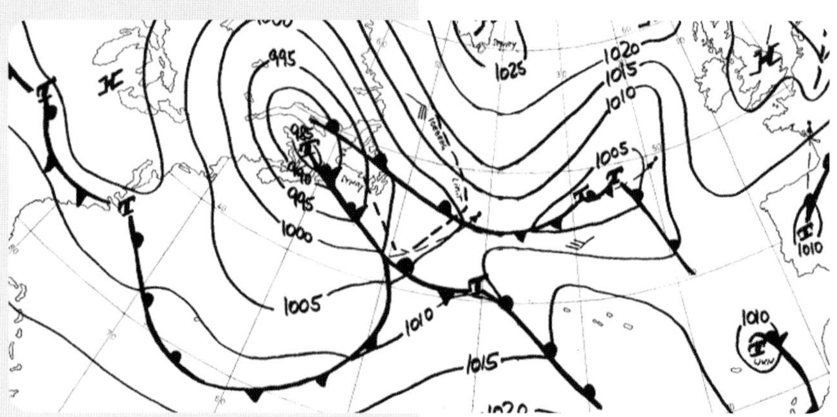

THE SORT OF BASIC WEATHER MAP THAT IS AVAILABLE FREE OF CHARGE.

When you start paying for forecasts, the difference is that you generally get someone interpreting the weather charts for you. A skilled forecaster can give you very specific weather information that focuses on your area and your timing. This is likely to be as good as it gets in terms of forecasting, but paying for this information means that you're not developing the skills to do it yourself. There are now specialist software programs that allow you to link in to weather information, either by email or by Internet connections, and these usually have excellent weather charts that show wind and sea conditions as well as the isobar charts.

Out at sea, you may not have access to the Internet and obtaining good weather forecasts can be more difficult. The facility for talking directly to the forecaster can be harder to achieve, but mobile phone links are improving and one system being developed will allow sophisticated weather information to be downloaded to a mobile phone. In general, when you are at sea you will have to focus on what free information is available by radio and then do your own interpretation. This will be a lot easier if you have studied the weather patterns before you leave and it is a good idea to practise relating forecasts to weather charts at all times, even when you have charts and telephone links available.

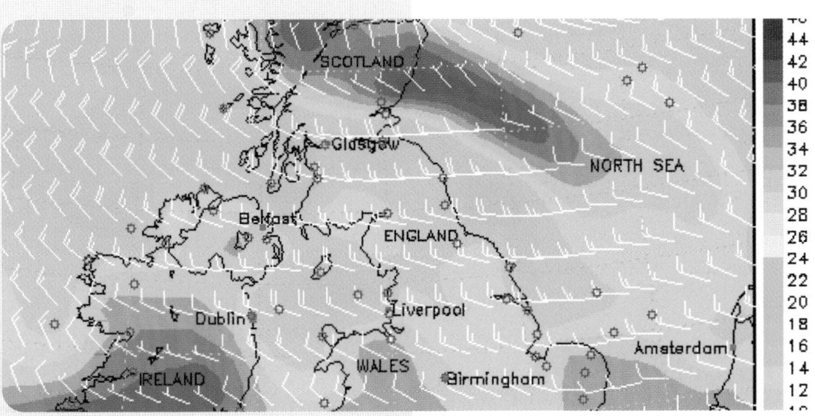

THE SORT OF SOPHISTICATED WEATHER MAP THAT TENDS TO COST MONEY BUT OFFERS EXTRA INFORMATION.

8 WEATHER FROM COAST STATIONS

Before you head out to sea, it may seem logical to phone a coastguard or other weather monitoring station along the coast to get an update on the actual weather at that location. The coast station will be able to provide you with the prevailing weather conditions and this can be a good way to check that the weather is actually following the forecaster's prediction. In a weather situation that is changing quite rapidly, such as when a front is passing through or when fog is forecast, the report from the coast station could provide a very useful update and help to put some timing on the changes.

However, use this type of information with caution. The report of the weather being experienced at the coast station may not reflect the general conditions prevailing out at sea. There can be two reasons for this; the first would simply be natural caution on the part of the reporter to exaggerate the weather conditions so that they cannot be accused of giving a misleading report. Better for them to make it sound as though the weather is worse than it really is, in case it does deteriorate quite rapidly, or just simply to introduce a note of caution. They won't want to be seen to encourage you to go to sea unless the conditions are benign. So, when they give the wind speed, they may give the maximum they have experienced, rather than the average. The wind speed in the gusts can be nearly twice the average wind speed and that could make a considerable difference to your plans, deterring you from going to sea even when the conditions are suitable.

Secondly, the wind at the coast station may not reflect what it's like out in the open sea. One reason for this is that the coast station may be situated on a headland quite high above the sea. Winds at sea level will not be as strong as those higher up, so the coast station will tend to record a higher wind speed in this situation. Another factor to take into consideration is that the wind always increases in strength around a high headland. This is because the airflow gets compressed as it is squeezed around the headland and this will increase the speed of the flow. A final factor to consider is that the coast station may be located on an upward slope of land and again this will tend to increase the wind speed if the wind is coming in off the sea.

All these factors tend to increase the wind speed recorded at a coast station so that wind reports from these locations will generally give a higher wind speed than may exist in the open sea – possibly as much as 10 knots higher, although this may not always be the case. There's no hard and fast rule about this, but if you do get a weather report from a coast station, treat it with a degree of caution.

A COAST STATION HIGH ON A HEADLAND IS UNLIKELY TO GIVE A RELIABLE IDEA OF WHAT THE WIND MIGHT BE LIKE AT SEA LEVEL.

9 RECORDING THE WEATHER

In any situation where you have to make decisions about the weather, or when you're developing your weather strategy, always write down the forecast if it is being received by radio or on TV (you can usually print out Internet forecasts for use later). Make a note of the forecast not only for the area you are or will be in, but also for the areas on either side.

With the forecast written down, you will be able to study it at leisure. This will allow you to interpret what the forecast is saying in more detail; in verbal forecasts, the forecaster tends to make every word used have significance, so make sure that you get it down word for word. Having the forecasts for either side of your area will also help you to build up a picture of what the weather is doing and you might be able to get a better indication of what is in store for the next 24 or 36 hours. Remember to write down such weather indicators as rain or showers because, while you may not be too worried about whether it is raining or not, these weather indicators

A CHART OF THE SHIPPING FORECAST AREAS IN NORTHERN EUROPE THAT CAN HELP YOU BUILD UP A PICTURE OF THE WEATHER FROM VERBAL FORECASTS.

can give you an idea about the movements of frontal systems.

If you're getting your weather information from the TV, forecasts will often show successive charts illustrating the movement of the weather systems. On the actual presentation on the TV, these tend to be shown too quickly for you to have time to study them in order to get a good picture of what the weather patterns are doing. If you have the facilities, record TV forecasts on video or DVD – this will allow you to play them back in slow motion in your own time and get a really good picture of the weather movements that are forecast. Remember, however, that TV forecasts tend to relate more to what is happening over the land than to conditions at sea, and many of the TV forecasts have given up showing the isobars and replaced them with fancy weather graphics, which will not always serve your purpose for a sea forecast.

There is no real substitute for proper weather charts when trying to understand the weather and this is where the Internet can be so valuable, but again do print out the forecast charts as well as studying them on the screen. It is now a legal requirement to get a forecast before going to sea, and a printed version serves as proof that you have done this.

10 READING BETWEEN THE LINES

Isobars – the lines you see on a weather chart – show the lines of equal atmospheric pressure. This in itself may not sound very exciting, but those lines contain a host of information about the weather. The lines connect places where equal barometric pressure is found or forecast, depending on the type of chart, and they form the basis of any weather forecast. Although they represent the atmospheric pressure, they are also the main indicator of wind strength and direction as well as showing the location of fronts, which can have a significant effect on the weather you will experience.

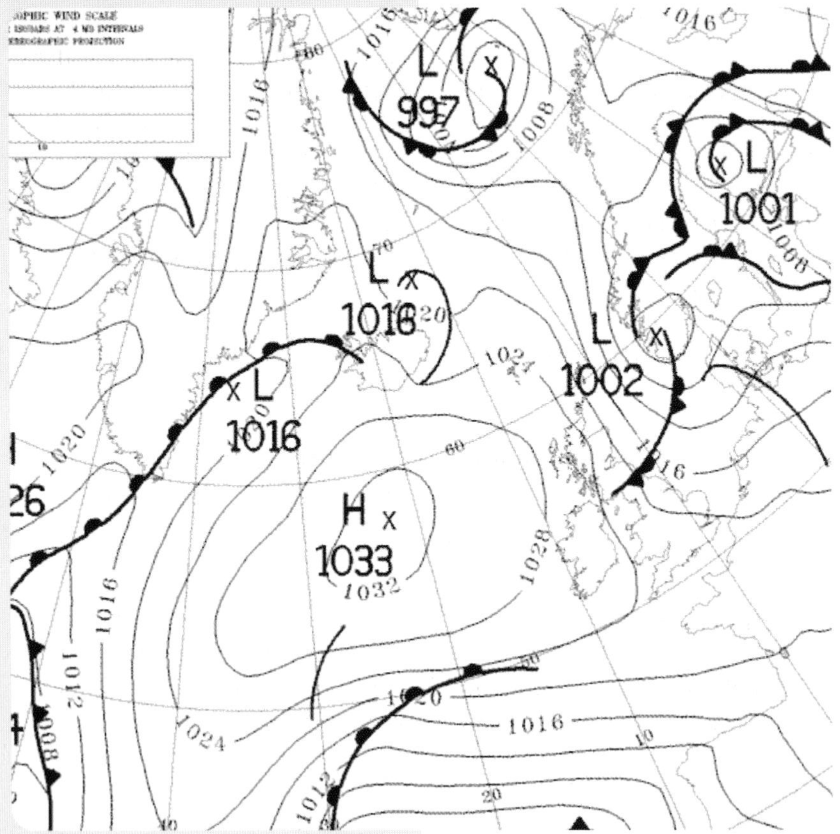

A FORECAST CHART WITH THE GRAPH IN THE TOP LEFT CORNER THAT ENABLES YOU TO CALCULATE WIND STRENGTH FROM THE DISTANCE BETWEEN THE ISOBARS.

It is the difference in pressure between adjacent locations that dictates what the wind strength will be, with the steeper pressure gradient indicating the stronger winds. So when the isobar lines are close together, the winds will be stronger; when they are further apart, weaker winds can be expected.

Because most weather charts are based on a Mercator projection similar to that used for most navigation charts, there will be distortion of the scale that will vary with latitude. This means that the distance between the isobars relating to an associated wind strength will also vary with latitude. To enable you to relate the distance between the isobars to the associated wind strength, the weather chart is provided with a scale. To find the related wind strength, measure the distance between the isobars in your location and read off the wind strength that relates that distance to your latitude.

You can also get an indication of the expected wind strength from the isobars. The air will tend to flow from an area of high pressure to an area of low pressure. However, it does not flow in a straight line because of the rotation of the earth, and the flow is more like water going down a plughole. The airflow will usually follow fairly closely the lines of the isobars, tending to flow more into the centre of a low pressure than along the direct line of the isobar.

In assessing the weather, it is mainly the variations in the distance apart of the direction of the lines that are important. Closely packed lines will indicate strong winds, and when they are wide apart you can expect weaker winds. Variations in the direction of the isobars could indicate the location of a front, when you can expect a change in wind direction. Also remember that the isobars you see on the chart are computer generated and averaged from the reported weather information. The scale of the charts tends to overlook any small local changes in the lines of the isobars, although these could have a significant impact on local weather.

Interpreting the isobar lines on the weather chart will give a good general idea of what to expect in terms of wind, but they don't necessarily tell the whole weather story.

11 THE MEANING OF 'LATER'

The word 'later' often features in weather forecasts, but like so much in this context it is an ill-defined word that could mean many things.

In trying to understand what 'later' means in the forecast, the first thing is to know the duration of the forecast you are being given. 'Later' is a relative term, suggesting that the events described will occur at some point in the second half of the forecast period. It is very common for a sea forecast to cover the next 24 hours, so here 'later' would mean an event occurring during the second 12 hour period of the forecast.

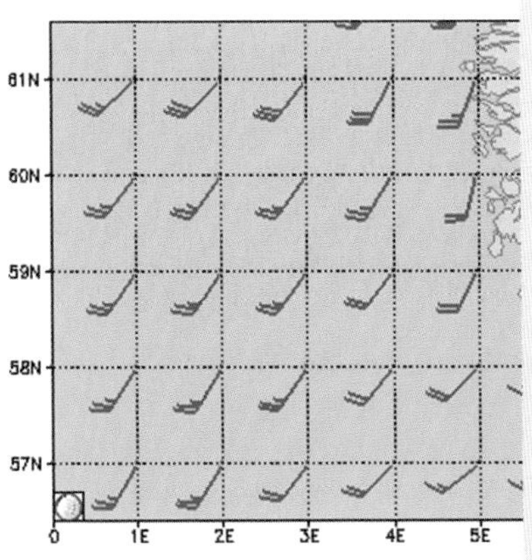

THESE ARE THE FORECAST WIND STRENGTHS FOR SEA AREA VIKING. OBVIOUSLY THE WINDS IN THE WEST WILL BE STRONGER THAN THOSE IN THE EAST, SHOWING HOW THE WEATHER IS MOVING.

For a weather feature to be happening 'later' suggests that the weather patterns are a moving event. Now, the sea area that is covered by the forecast may be quite considerable, covering an area extending perhaps for 500-650km (300-400 miles). If the weather is moving through that sea area, your position within the area will have a considerable bearing on when that 'later' period occurs.

Weather patterns may move at speeds of anywhere between, say, 10 and 40 knots, so it will take on average perhaps 10 hours for a forecast change to move through your particular sea area. It could be longer, it could be less, but if you have an understanding of the weather patterns you should have some idea of the speed of change. You'll know where you are within the given forecast sea area, so you should be able to fine-tune the meaning of 'later'. If you are at the point in the sea area where the weather system first approaches, 'later' is likely to mean within the next 6 hours. If you are on the far side, it could mean up to 24 hours. From this you can see how important it can be to fine-tune the weather forecast with your own interpretation.

THE SPEED OF THE WEATHER 12

Knowing the speed and direction of the movement of weather systems is one of the most important factors in weather forecasting. In some situations, weather changes take place at quite predictable speeds, which can be a great help in forecasting what lies ahead, but in other situations there can be uncertainty. In relation to speed, the changes that can be predicted most accurately are those associated with low-pressure systems. It is generally these that bring the bad weather you are trying to avoid, and knowing the speed of their progress can be a great help in predicting timing.

The forecast chart will show the direction in which a low pressure is expected to travel and you can measure the speed of travel from consecutive weather charts. As a general rule, the deeper the low-pressure system, the faster it will move, so a weak system may move at 10 knots while a deeper, more active low could move at 30 knots or more.

Very active weather fronts usually move the fastest; they tend to swing out in a curve from the centre of the low and move faster than the low-pressure area itself, because they are swinging around the centre as well as moving forward with the low-pressure centre. This means that an active weather front could be moving at 40 knots or more.

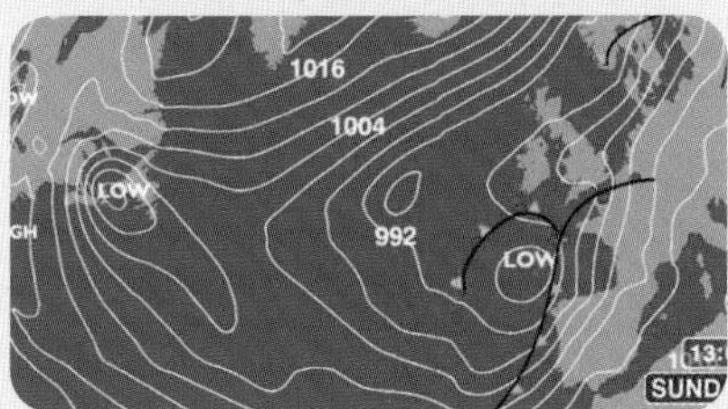

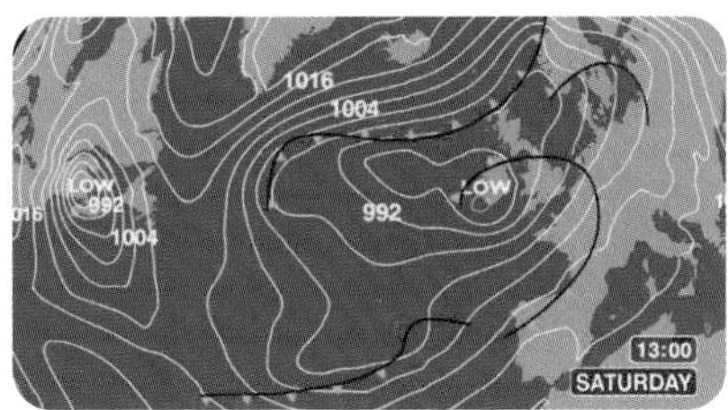

YOU CAN GET SOME IDEA OF THE SPEED OF THE WEATHER FROM TWO CONSECUTIVE WEATHER CHARTS.

13 PINNING DOWN THE WIND STRENGTH

Knowing the wind direction is important to your weather strategy and planning, but the most important factor in any forecast will be the strength of the wind. The wind strength will largely determine what is practical and possible with regard to your plans to go to sea, but unfortunately this is the factor where the forecasters can be rather vague. Forecasts will often predict a range of wind strengths with 10 knots or more difference between the highest and the lowest of the forecast wind speeds. That level of wind speed variation is not sufficiently accurate for passage planning requirements, because while the lower wind speed level may allow fine sailing, the upper speed level could be untenable. However, you can upgrade the wind strength accuracy of the forecast with your own interpretation of the situation.

We have already seen that one forecast sea area can cover a considerable distance, perhaps 300 or 400 miles or more. If you look at this forecast area on the weather chart, you may be aware of how the distance between the isobar lines changes over the forecast area in which you are interested. If the isobars are closer together in your particular position than they are in the other parts of the forecast area, then you can assume that you will experience wind speeds at the top end of the forecast range. Conversely, if the lines are further apart in your position, you can expect winds to be at the lower end of the forecast speed range.

You can often get a better idea of the wind strengths you might experience by looking at the forecast wind strength in the adjacent forecast sea areas. This is even more relevant if you happen to be close to the edge of one forecast area – what is going in the adjacent sea area can be equally significant, particularly if the weather patterns are coming from that area. If, for example, you look at the English Channel, which is divided into four sea areas, what is going on in the western sea areas will give you a good idea of what wind strengths to expect if you are in the eastern sea areas.

In order to pin down the wind strength more accurately in this way, you need also to be aware that the weather patterns will most likely be moving, generally from west to east. An area where the distance between the isobars is less could later become an area where the isobars are closer together, suggesting that the wind will increase in strength during the forecast period. If you have consecutive weather charts available, you'll be able to get a good picture of when and how the wind strengths will change. It is when you are having to rely on verbal or text weather information, such as that given over the radio, that you will need to interpret the forecast to get a better and more reliable idea of how the wind strength will develop and change.

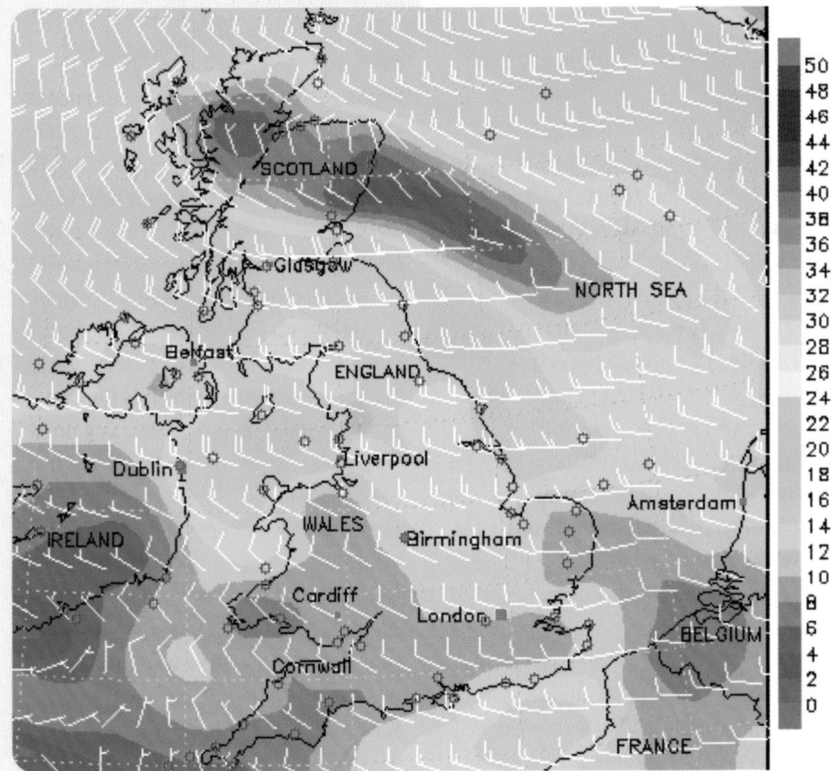

A CHART OF THE SHIPPING FORECAST AREAS IN NORTHERN EUROPE THAT CAN HELP YOU BUILD UP A PICTURE OF THE WEATHER FROM VERBAL FORECASTS.

14 THE LANGUAGE OF FORECASTS

MARINE FORECASTS GLOSSARY

Marine forecasts contain a number of terms that are used to convey specific meanings.

Gale Warnings

- Gale – Winds of at least Beaufort force 8 (34-40 knots) or gusts reaching 43-51 knots
- Severe gale – Winds of force 9 (41-47 knots) or gusts reaching 52-60 knots
- Storm – Winds of force 10 (48-55 knots) or gusts reaching 61-68 knots
- Violent storm – Winds of force 11 (56-63 knots) or gusts of 69 knots or more
- Hurricane force – Winds of force 12 (64 knots or more)

Note: *The term used is 'hurricane force'; the term 'hurricane' on its own means a true tropical cyclone, not experienced in British waters.*

Timings

- Imminent – Expected within six hours of time of issue
- Soon – Expected within six to 12 hours of time of issue
- Later – Expected more than 12 hours from time of issue

Visibility

- Fog – Visibility less than 1,000 metres (approx 1,100 yards)
- Poor – Visibility between 1,000 metres (approx 1,100 yards) and 2 nautical miles
- Moderate – Visibility between 2 and 5 nautical miles
- Good – Visibility more than 5 nautical miles

Movement of Pressure Systems

- Slowly – Moving at less than 15 knots
- Steadily – Moving at 15-25 knots
- Rather quickly - Moving at 25-35 knots
- Rapidly – Moving at 35-45 knots
- Very rapidly – Moving at more than 45 knots

Pressure Tendency in Station Reports

- Rising (or falling) slowly – Pressure change of 0.1-1.5 hPa in the preceding three hours
- Rising (or falling) – Pressure change of 1.6-3.5 hPa in the preceding three hours
- Rising (or falling) quickly – Pressure change of 3.6-6.0 hPa in the preceding three hours
- Rising (or falling) very rapidly – Pressure change of more than 6.0 hPa in the preceding three hours
- Now rising (or falling) – Pressure has been falling [rising] or steady in the preceding three hours, but at the time of observation was definitely rising [falling]

Note: *For those more familiar with the millibar, 1 hPa = 1 mb*

Wind

- Wind direction – Indicates the direction from which the wind is blowing
- Becoming cyclonic – Indicates that there will be considerable change in wind direction across the path of a depression within the forecast area
- Veering – The changing of the wind direction clockwise, eg SW to W
- Backing – The changing of the wind direction anticlockwise, eg SE to NE

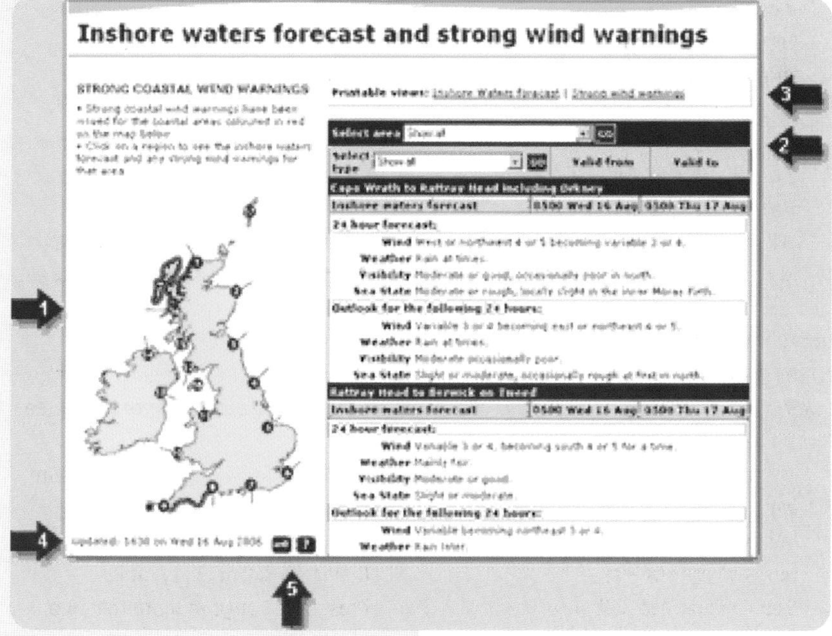

A BASIC INTERNET FORECAST, FOR WHICH YOU NEED TO KNOW THE LANGUAGE OF THE FORECASTERS.

15 FORECASTING WAVE HEIGHT

Of particular interest to powerboat drivers, and to a lesser extent to sailors, will be the size of the waves generated by the wind. The size, direction and gradient of a wave tend to dictate both the comfort level on board and the speed of progress. However, except in open ocean areas, the weather forecasts tend to shy away from giving information about wave heights and direction. This is because the size of the waves, and particularly their gradients, will be affected by several external factors which are not related directly to the wind strength, so forecasting inshore waves can be very difficult and there will tend to be short-term changes. The Beaufort Scale (see pages 44-5) gives an indication of the size of open-ocean waves that can be expected with certain wind strengths, so if you know the forecast wind strength, you'll have an idea of what waves to expect. In the ocean the wind is virtually the only factor that will affect wave size, apart from the time lag that occurs between the wind freshening and the waves rising to match.

In inshore waters, several other factors come into play. The waves will be smaller under the shelter of the land where the fetch - the distance from the

WAVE HEIGHTS IN INSHORE WATERS CAN VARY CONSIDERABLY DEPENDING ON DEPTH, TOPOGRAPHY AND FETCH.

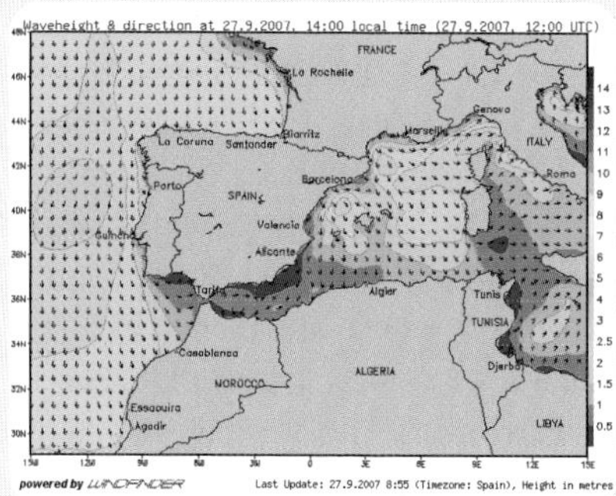

A WESTERN MEDITERRANEAN WAVE FORECAST CHART.

land to your position in the direction from which the wind is blowing - is reduced. There are tables that show this difference and these give a guide of what you might expect.

In tidal waters (which applies to most inshore waters), the direction and strength of the tidal flow will have an impact on wave size and gradient. The waves will be lower when wind and tide are both from the same direction and higher and steeper when the wind and tide are in opposition. Any tidal flow over 1 knot is likely to have a significant effect on the waves and this will be exaggerated around headlands, where both the wind strength and the tidal flow tend to increase as they are compressed by the headland. Many well-known tidal races exist in these conditions and can generate quite dangerous sea conditions, even in modest winds.

You can see the effect of the tidal flow by studying the tidal atlas in conjunction with the forecast wind direction. The actual effect on the waves is not always easy to forecast, with some very local changes occurring, and the differences in height and gradient can only really be assessed from experience. Generally though, the stronger the tidal flow, the higher and steeper the waves when wind and tide are in opposition.

Waves will also tend to be higher when they encounter shallow water and here, the bigger the waves, the deeper the water in which you can expect to experience this phenomenon. These aspects are dealt with in more detail in the chapter The wind and the sea (pages 44-61), but they are brought in here as part of the business of translating the forecast into the conditions you will experience when you are out at sea.

16 FINE-TUNING FACTORS

Fine-tuning largely involves changing the general forecast for a considerable sea area into a specific forecast for your locality. The two factors to be taken into account are timing and position.

The forecast will give a general indication of when changes in the weather will pass through the region of the forecast, but you are specifically interested in when they will pass your position or your future position. A study of the weather chart will help here; but remember that weather charts are only updated every 12 hours, and during these forecast periods the relative positions of frontal systems, high and low pressure areas and isobars could change considerably, particularly with a fast-moving weather system.

You should gain a clearer indication of the timing of changes by observing the weather and clouds being experienced where you are. This is covered in more detail in the chapter Local weather conditions (pages 62 – 81) and will certainly give you a better idea of what is going on, particularly if there is a frontal system passing through. However, it isn't likely to give you much idea about wind strengths and the timing of changes – you need to rely on the forecast for that. You should also consider the effect of tidal flow changes – while the main effect will be on the waves, strong tides can affect the wind strength as the water flow drags the surface wind along.

Knowing your position relative to the forecast region will also help in fine-tuning. If you are close to the edge that will be first affected by changes, expect things to change before the time that the forecast suggests. At the opposite extremity, expect changes after the forecast time. Checking the forecasts for the areas either side of your region will also help you anticipate the timing of any changes.

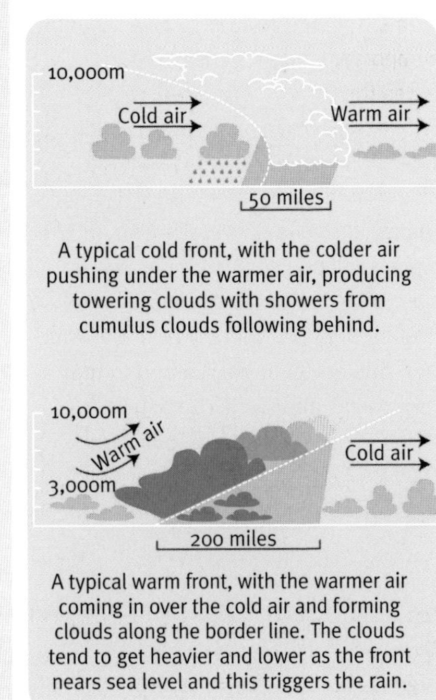

A typical cold front, with the colder air pushing under the warmer air, producing towering clouds with showers from cumulus clouds following behind.

A typical warm front, with the warmer air coming in over the cold air and forming clouds along the border line. The clouds tend to get heavier and lower as the front nears sea level and this triggers the rain.

INCONSISTENCIES IN THE FORECAST 17

When obtaining a weather forecast, particularly the text or verbal type, remember that the forecaster will only give a general indication of the average conditions likely to be experienced over a considerable sea area. Even when you have a weather chart available, you will find that the isobar lines are computer-generated and flow in a smooth pattern that represents the average, based on readings from weather reports. This will meet most of the requirements for forecast purposes, but might hide some local inconsistencies.

These inconsistencies can take three forms. The shortest-term are the temporary gusts and lulls that occur when the wind increases or decreases briefly around the average. These are nearly impossible to forecast, and while they are more likely to be found close to land, they can also be experienced in the open sea. The potential doubling of the wind speed in a gust can be a significant factor for sailboats. Another form of inconsistency occurs in association with rain squalls or thunderstorms, which can also be very localised. These are covered in more detail in Squalls, 37 and Thunderstorms, 38, and are mainly caused by local atmospheric disturbances caused by a rise in termperature. The effects can last for up to an hour or so and again see a significant increase in wind strength. A prolonged wind increase could bring about a change in sea conditions but this is unlikely to be major, although the longer-term nature of a squall can certainly affect sailing performance.

Finally, there is the inconsistency that is created when the isobars do not follow the smooth, tidy lines shown on the weather charts. There will be local areas where the lines are temporarily closer together or wider apart and this is likely to cause increases or decreases in the general wind strength.

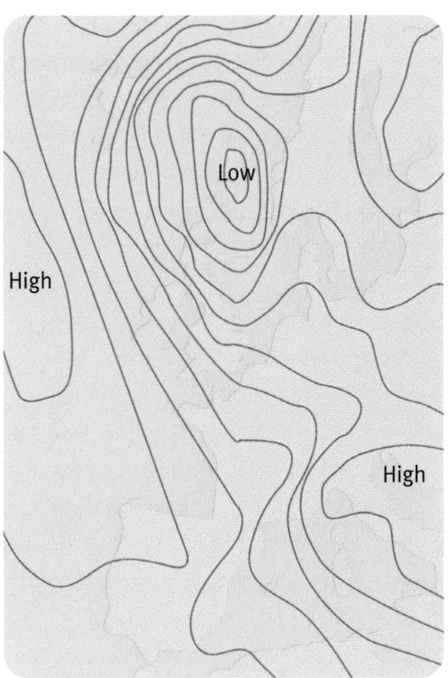

THE DISTANCE BETWEEN THE ISOBARS CAN OFTEN VARY CONSIDERABLY IN QUITE LOCAL AREAS, LEADING TO LOCAL CHANGES IN WIND STRENGTH.

18 WHEN THE AIRFLOW IS BROKEN

It is not too difficult to picture what happens when the regular flow of air generated by the wind encounters something in its path. There is no visible evidence of the turbulence that can be generated by the interruption in flow (unless it is affecting clouds, and even then it is relatively slow motion), but it can have a significant effect on local weather conditions.

You can get an idea of the way in which the airflow is affected if you look at the water flowing downstream from the pillars of a bridge in a river. Here you can see the way in which eddies are formed in the interrupted flow and where, in places, the flow can actually be reversed or turn in a circular pattern over short distances. The same sort of thing happens in the air, but the effects will be felt over a larger area than that seen on the water and could extend for several kilometres rather than several metres.

You tend to get this broken airflow when the wind is off the land. You don't get features like a bridge pillar standing up into the air stream out at sea, except perhaps a tall isolated rock; it is more a case of the air flow over the land becoming complicated by flowing over uneven topography. Think of it more in terms of water flowing over a very uneven river bed. There is also the fact that, unlike a bridge pillar standing in the water where the water can only flow round it, the air is flowing both over and round the obstruction or the land so that the patterns of flow become more complex.

The result will be a considerable variation in wind strengths and directions in a localised area and you can't expect the weather forecast to show these local variations. The effect on the wind when it is flowing over or from the land or islands will mainly occur when the wind is off the land, but there can also be significant interruptions when the wind is flowing along the coast and any localized changes are likely to be exaggerated when the land is high or very irregular.

Some of the more specific effects that can be found, such as considerably increased wind strengths and squalls, are explored in When the wind is off the land, 19, Winds around and over islands, 20 and Winds parallel to the shore, 21, and understanding and anticipating these effects can increase both your pleasure and safety at sea. These local interruptions or changes in the wind patterns are likely to be much more significant for sailboats than for powerboats.

THE WIND OVER THESE MOUNTAINS IS CREATING A DISTURBED AIRFLOW, LEADING TO THE FORMATION OF THE DARK CLOUDS.

19 WHEN THE WIND IS OFF THE LAND

When the wind is flowing from land to sea, you can expect good sea conditions when you are running close to the land because the fetch is small with the land providing good shelter. The distance offshore in which you can expect to find these slight sea conditions will depend on the strength of the wind, with a strong wind starting to generate rough seas within 3km (2 miles) or so of the coast. If you stick close inshore, you can expect to find the moderate sea conditions that are fine for a powerboat, but in a sailboat you might experience a variety of unexpected wind conditions.

A lot will depend on the topography of the land. When you have valleys or river estuaries running down to the sea, you can expect to find stronger winds in the areas where these valleys meet the sea. The wind will tend to accelerate down the valleys and it could be a couple of numbers higher on the Beaufort Scale in the areas where low land meets the sea.

The effect of these local valley winds is likely to be more severe when it is a cold wind blowing in from the north, as the cold wind with its higher density will tend to flow into the valleys and accelerate. This can be seen on a large scale with the Mistral winds that blow down the Rhône valley in the South of France, but you will also find this effect in much smaller valleys.

You might expect a relatively steady flow of wind down the valleys when the wind is off the land, but under the higher ground between the valleys you could find some unexpected wind shifts. Here the wind will blow off the top of the cliff and want to drop down to sea level, creating some back eddies where the wind direction is reversed over local areas. The wind coming out of the valleys is also likely to spread out once it encounters the open sea and this could create a local wind parallel to the coast as it swings round to try to fill the vacuum under the higher ground.

These local changes in wind direction and possible strength can be difficult to cope with when you are sailing and the changes can be quite quick and very local. When the wind is strong, the changes in wind direction and strength are likely to be more intense and there is the possibility of sudden squalls where contrary winds meet.

In strong to gale force wind conditions off the land where the wind has blown over high land close inland, you could find that it comes down steep valleys in the form of squalls. These can be quite vicious rotating squalls, like eddies found in an interrupted water flow, and they can come screaming across the water in what looks like a white-out before dying out offshore.

So running inshore in strong winds is likely to give you the sort of slight sea conditions that you may want, but you can expect the wind to come from unexpected directions and to vary considerably in strength. For smoother sailing, keeping further offshore could give you more predictable winds.

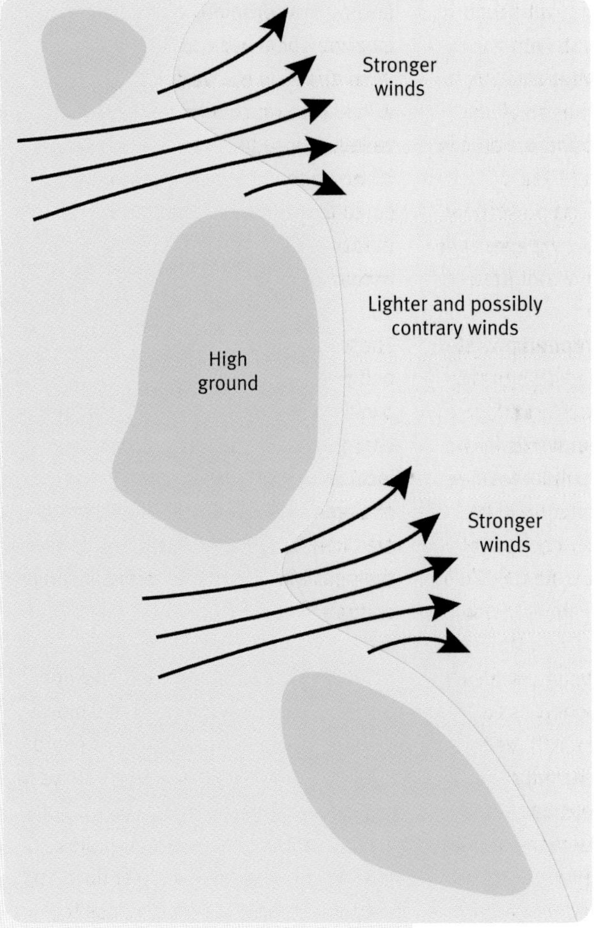

WHEN THE WIND IS COMING OFF THE LAND THERE CAN BE SIGNIFICANT CHANGES IN THE WIND STRENGTH AND DIRECTION FOR 2 OR 3 MILES OFF THE COAST.

20 WINDS AROUND AND OVER ISLANDS

It is easy to imagine that, if you are looking for shelter, holing up in the lee of an island could be a good idea. However, the wind has a knack of invading areas of apparent shelter like this and creating some unsettled and difficult conditions. Finding shelter in this way could work with larger islands where the land mass is large enough to be like mainland, but smaller islands may not offer the shelter you are looking for.

If we go back to the analogy in When the airflow is broken, 18, with water flowing round a bridge pillar in a river, it shouldn't be too difficult to imagine the type of wind eddies that could be generated in the lee of an island. However, the flow of wind over and round an island will be more like that found with water flowing over a large rock on the river bed. Not only can the wind come from unpredictable directions but the flow can be both reversed and increased, with the distinct possibility of serious wind squalls that can produce some quite disturbing conditions.

The wind flow around an island can become quite confused – not only is the wind coming around the sides of the island, but you also need to consider the wind that has been forced up and over the island. This adds a third dimension of turbulence that will mix with the side flow, so in the lee you can find very unpredictable wind conditions.

A lot will depend on the size and shape of the island in question. The wind eddies are likely to be much more severe around small, steep-sided islands, which will cause the maximum interruption to the airflow. The effects will also be much more noticeable in strong winds, say those over force 5, which of course are the sort of conditions in which you might be thinking of finding shelter. Below this wind strength threshold, any wind eddies are likely to be relatively weak and they could well die out rapidly before having any significant effect.

When sailing past an island, it can pay to pass some distance off to avoid this sort of turbulence. In a powerboat you might also want to keep clear of the lee side in stronger winds, because the waves approaching the weather side can be refracted around the island and meet as crossing waves on the lee side, generating difficult clapotic seas. By and large, then, islands are places that you want to give a wide berth in stronger winds, although the conditions around low-lying islands will tend to be less severe and once the island is, say, 8km (5 miles) across or more, the chances of the difficult turbulence and conditions will be reduced.

WINDS AROUND AND OVER ISLANDS

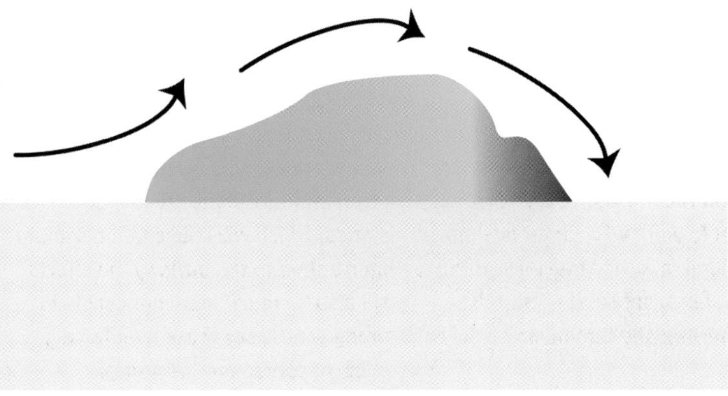

Winds over an island

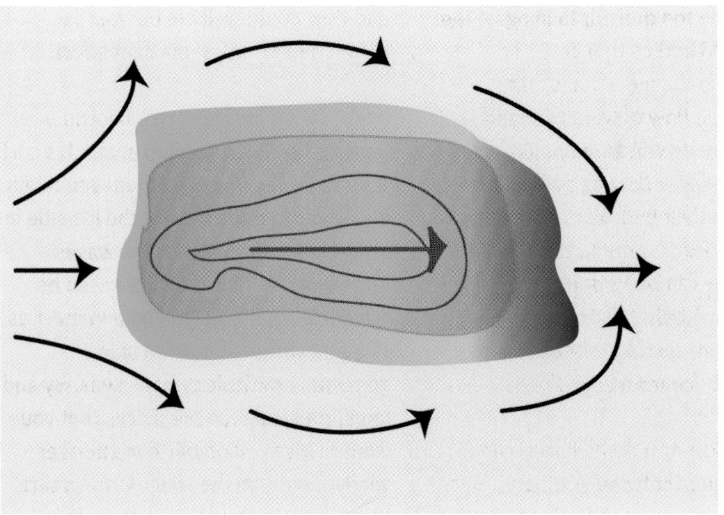

Winds around an island

THIS DIAGRAM SHOWS THE TYPICAL AIRFLOW OVER AND AROUND AN ISLAND AND SHOWS WHY YOU MIGHT EXPECT TURBULENCE ON THE LEE SIDE.

21 WINDS PARALLEL TO THE SHORE

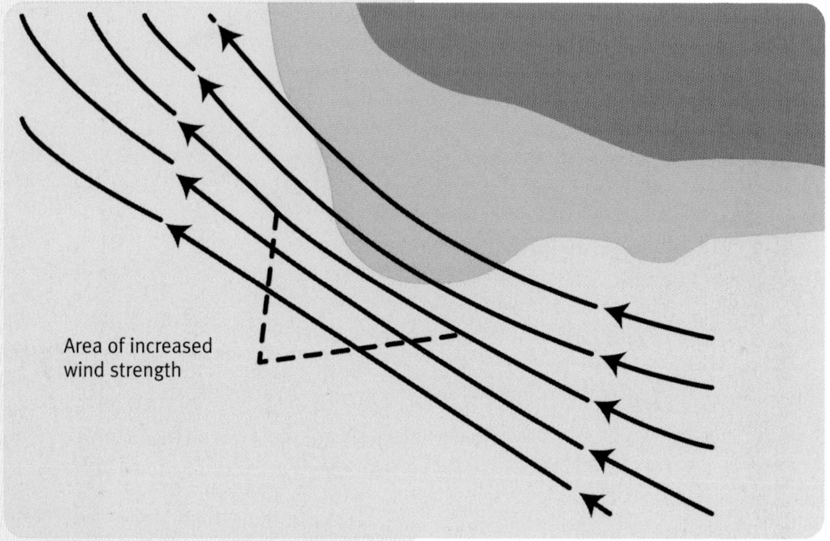

WIND SWEEPING PAST A HEADLAND TENDS TO CONTOUR ROUND THE END OF THE HEADLAND EVEN WHEN THE LAND IS LOW LYING. THIS TENDS TO COMPRESS THE AIR FLOW, GIVING STRONGER WINDS AROUND THE HEADLAND.

When the wind is blowing along or close to the line of the shore, there can be areas where you will find stronger or lighter winds. Some of these effects will be caused by the topography and others will be the result of differences between the wind over the land and that over the sea. The wind finds less resistance when it is flowing over the sea than where it is flowing over the land, because the sea surface is generally relatively smooth compared with the surface of the land.

You will almost certainly get stronger winds around a pronounced headland when the wind is flowing along the coastline. It's easy to imagine how the headland interferes with the steady flow of the wind, which is forced to go round or over it. Either way the airflow is compressed, leaving less space for the air to flow through. When that happens, the airflow inevitably speeds up so the wind will be stronger in these areas. The higher and more pronounced the headland, the greater the likely strengthening of the wind that will occur. Even with quite low-lying headlands you are likely to find an increase in the wind strength at sea level.

Then there are the factors of divergence and convergence, terms that relate to the way in which the wind direction is changed when it flows from land to sea or vice versa. This means that the wind will generally be blowing in a different direction over the land than over the sea. There can be a difference of as much as 30 degrees between the two, with the wind over the land always being more clockwise or a higher direction than the sea wind.

When the land wind and the sea wind are flowing in a converging direction along the coast, this will lead to a strengthening of the wind. When they are flowing away from each other, the wind strength will reduce. If you stand with your back to the direction of the wind and the land is on your right-hand side, you can expect the coastal winds to be stronger. With the land on your left, expect weaker winds.

To a certain extent, this will seem rather like the effect you can get with sea breezes. The big difference between the two types of wind is that with convergent and divergent winds, the increases and decreases in wind speed are not dependent on the time of day; however sea breezes are, and you can encounter them during both day and night.

22 SEA BREEZES

Sea breezes are a well-known phenomenon that can turn the predicted wind on its head and create some uncertain and unpredictable conditions. They are probably the most tricky wind situation that you will have to deal with when cruising or racing along a coastline in a sailboat and their strength and effect will vary with the prevailing conditions.

In learning to understand sea breezes, we must first look at how they are created. The primary cause is the land heating up in the daytime. The land will invariably heat up more quickly than the sea; the wind over the land rises as it is heated, causing cooler air from over the sea to be sucked in at low level to fill the void created by the rising air. This air coming in from seaward is the sea breeze – hence its name – but the rising warm air over the land will cool as it rises and in doing so it tends to flow out to sea and drop.

Eventually, once the sea breeze becomes fully established, a circular airflow is created, with cooler upper air flowing out to seaward to replace the air being sucked in by the rising warm air over the land. This circuit of warming and cooling is a small, self-contained weather system in its own right and it usually starts up after midday when the land has warmed up considerably.

There are two things to note about sea breezes. The first is that they are only likely to be felt up to about 8km (5 miles) offshore. Secondly, their effect on the prevailing wind will depend on the direction of this prevailing wind. If it is coming in off the sea and blowing towards the shore, then it will be strengthened by the sea breeze. Conversely, if the prevailing wind is off the land then the two winds could possibly cancel each other out or there could be a reversal of wind direction. Much will depend on the relative strengths of two winds.

The situation gets more complex when the wind is flowing along the coast. Again, the relative strengths of the two winds will determine the actual wind direction that will prevail. In calm conditions a sea breeze is likely to be around force 3 or 4, so a wind along the coast at the same strength would produce a resultant wind at an angle of about 45 degrees to the coastline. Stronger winds will increase this angle and lesser winds will reduce it, but it is very hard to calculate just what the final effect is likely to be.

Sea breezes will die out an hour or two before the sun sets, and if the land cools quickly then the reverse effect could manifest, with a wind flowing from the land to the sea. You're only likely to get sea breezes of any significance in the summer when the sun is hot enough to heat the land to a temperature considerably higher than the sea. The presence of a sea breeze can often be detected as a line of cloud over the coastline indicating where the rising air over the land is being cooled as it rises.

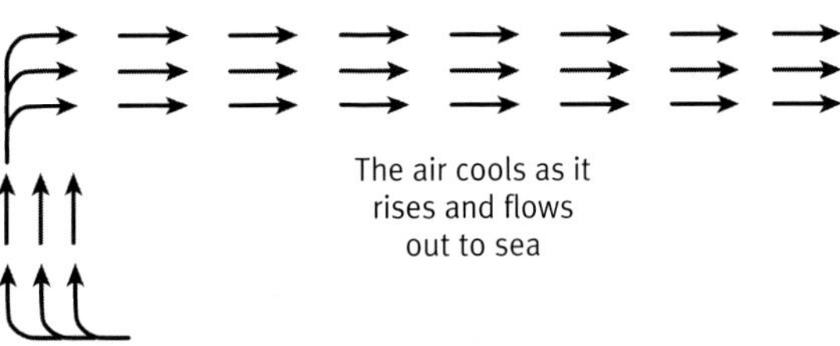

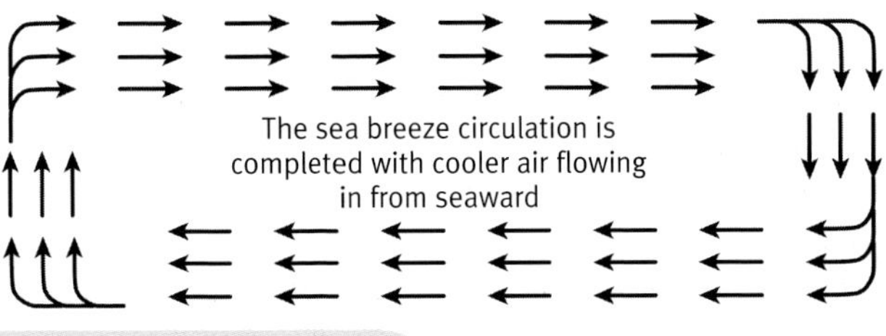

THE SEQUENCE OF EVENTS THAT CAN LEAD TO A SEA BREEZE DEVELOPING.

23 THE BEAUFORT SCALE

BEAUFORT SCALE NUMBER KNOTS	MEAN WIND SPEED KNOTS	LIMITS OF WIND SPEED	DESCRIPTION	SEA CRITERIA
0	00	LESS THAN 1	CALM	SEA LIKE A MIRROR.
1	02	1 - 3	LIGHT AIR	RIPPLES WITH THE APPEARANCE OF SCALES BUT WITHOUT FOAM CRESTS.
2	05	4 - 6	LIGHT BREEZE	SMALL WAVELETS, STILL SHORT BUT MORE PRONOUNCED. CRESTS HAVE A GLASSY APPEARANCE BUT DO NOT BREAK.
3	09	7 - 10	GENTLE BREEZE	LARGE WAVELETS. CRESTS BEGIN TO BREAK. FOAM OF GLASSY APPEARANCE. PERHAPS SCATTERED WHITE HORSES.
4	13	11 - 16	MODERATE BREEZE	SMALL WAVES, BECOMING LONGER. FAIRLY FREQUENT WHITE HORSES.
5	19	17 - 21	FRESH BREEZE	MODERATE WAVES TAKING A MORE PRONOUNCED LONG FORM. MANY WHITE HORSES ARE FORMED.
6	24	22 - 27	STRONG BREEZE	LARGE WAVES BEGIN TO FORM. WHITE FOAM CRESTS ARE MORE EXTENSIVE EVERYWHERE AND PROBABLY SOME SPRAY.
7	30	28 - 33	NEAR GALE	SEA HEAPS UP AND WHITE FOAM FROM BREAKING WAVES BEGINS TO BE BLOWN IN STREAKS ALONG THE DIRECTION OF THE WIND.
8	37	34 - 40	GALE	MODERATELY HIGH WAVES OF GREATER LENGTH. EDGES OF CRESTS BEGIN TO BREAK INTO SPINDRIFT. THE FOAM IS BLOWN IN WELL-MARKED STREAKS ALONG THE DIRECTION OF THE WIND.
9	44	41 - 47	STRONG GALE	HIGH WAVES AND DENSE STREAKS OF FOAM ALONG THE DIRECTION OF THE WIND. CRESTS OF WAVES BEGIN TO TOPPLE, TUMBLE AND ROLL OVER. SPRAY MAY AFFECT VISIBILITY.
10	52	48 - 55	STORM	VERY HIGH WAVES WITH LONG OVERHANGING CRESTS. THE RESULTING FOAM IS BLOWN IN DENSE WHITE STREAKS ALONG THE DIRECTION OF THE WIND. THE SURFACE OF THE SEA TAKES A WHITE APPEARANCE AND THE TUMBLING OF THE SEA BECOMES HEAVY AND SHOCK LIKE. VISIBILITY AFFECTED.

THE BEAUFORT SCALE

The Beaufort Scale works in two ways. If you know the wind speed, it will indicate the sort of sea conditions that might be associated with that wind speed. Alternatively, if you know the sea conditions being experienced, then it will give you an idea of the associated wind speed. It presupposes that you know one of these two factors, the wind strength or the sea conditions, and it enables you to gauge the other. So the Beaufort Scale is really a translation table, which has alternative uses in port and out at sea.

In harbour, the main use of the Beaufort Scale will be to give you an idea of what sea conditions you might encounter in relation to the forecast wind speed. This method of translating the forecast wind speed or wind force into sea conditions is very useful and with experience you will do this almost automatically, without reference to the table.

Most weather forecasts still use the Beaufort Scale numbers when describing the wind strength because one number covers a range of wind speeds, making the forecast simpler.

When the forecast quotes two Beaufort numbers, say force 3 to 4, this covers a much wider range of wind speeds, and this can mean that there is considerable vagueness about the forecast wind strength. It implies that the range of wind speeds could cover anything between 7 knots and 16 knots; however, it is more likely to mean that the wind strength will be at the top end of the force 3 range or at the bottom end of the force 4 range, around 10 or 11 knots. Of course it could also mean that the wind will be force 3 in one part of the forecast area and force 4 in another. This example demonstrates the weakness of the Beaufort Scale when the wind speed is at the cusp between two wind strengths.

24 THE EFFECT OF WIND ON THE TIDES

At first glance there does not appear to be any reason why the wind should affect the tides, but it does so in two ways. There is the effect of the wind on the tidal streams and then there is the effect of the wind on the height of the tide. As in most situations where the wind is involved, the effects will be more noticeable when the wind is stronger.

First let us look at the effect on the tidal streams. The tidal stream is a mass of flowing water, strongest in the middle of the stream but slowed at the edges where it comes into contact with shallower water or the land. The wind is in direct contact with this flowing water at the surface and it is not hard to visualise the effect. When the wind is blowing with the tide, the tidal stream will flow stronger at the surface and this effect will be felt a metre (3ft) or so down, in the region of the water where boats operate.

You get the reverse when the wind is blowing against the tidal stream - this will slow the flow down. Even in strong winds, the effect of the wind on the tide is unlikely to be more than 1 knot, so it shouldn't have a major effect on your navigation. It is only in narrow channels that the effect is likely to be significant; but then you'll be travelling in the same direction as the tide and not across it.

There will also be an effect on the height of the tide and this is partly because the increase in the tidal flow will result in a surge when the tide is flowing stronger, leading to a build-up of water and resulting in higher than predicted tides. This surge effect is likely to be felt in strong winds that have been blowing from the same direction for some time and, even if there are not strong winds in your area, winds within 160km (100 miles) or so could cause this surge effect. There can be lower than predicted tides when the wind is flowing against the tidal stream.

The other cause for the tidal surge is that the stronger winds will often be associated with a depression or low-pressure area, giving the tides more freedom to rise higher because the atmospheric pressure is less. It will take quite a deep low to have a significant effect on the tide and then it could be in the order of 1m (3ft) higher or lower than predicted.

Because both of these phenomena are associated with strong winds, they are less likely to affect your boating plans. The effect on the tidal streams is not likely to have a significant impact on navigation and the difference in tidal height is only likely to be significant when you are entering a tidal harbour.

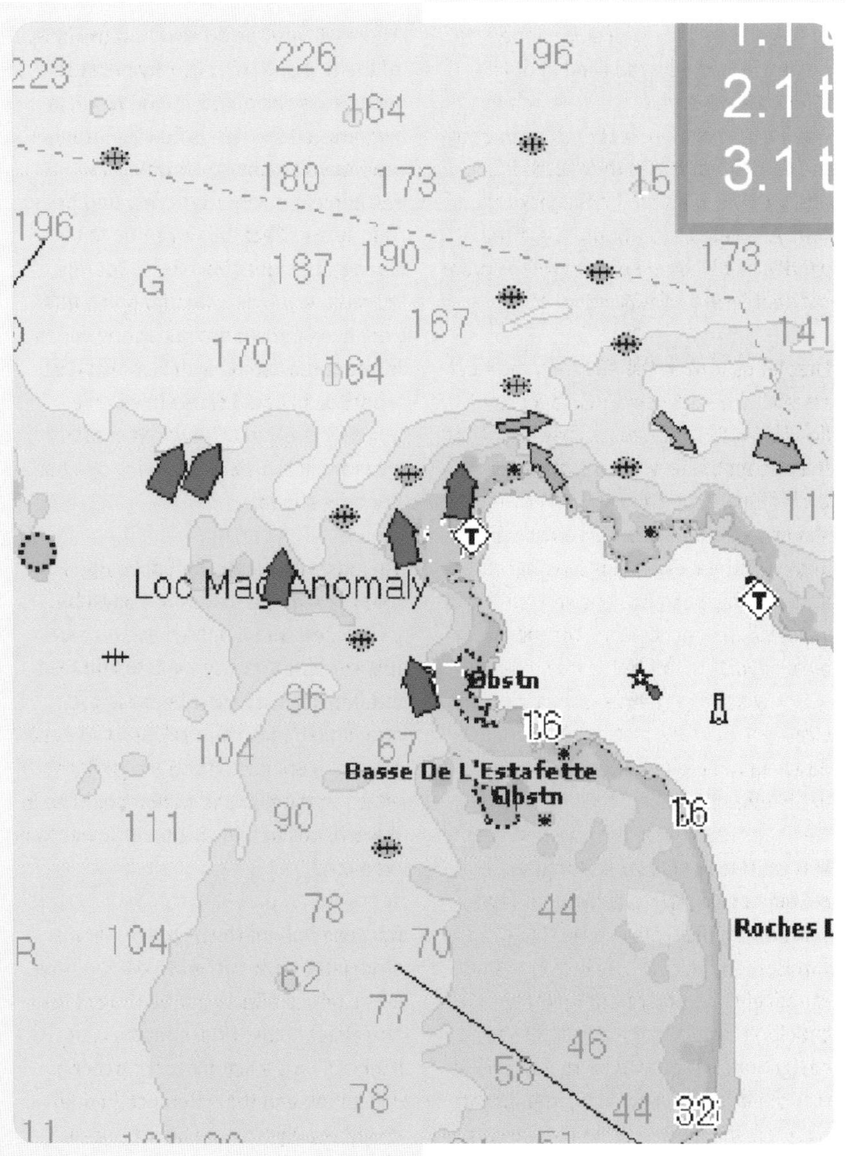

THE LARGE RED ARROWS ON THIS CHART SHOW THE EXPECTED TIDES, BUT THESE CAN CHANGE IN STRENGTH WITH CHANGES IN THE WIND.

25 TIDES AND WAVES

A WIND AGAINST TIDE SEA FORMED IN A HARBOUR ENTRANCE.

The tide can have a significant effect on the kind of waves you experience and the change in conditions as the tide changes can be dramatic. The main effect is that it will shorten the wavelength, and this will make the waves steeper and more difficult to negotiate.

When the wind and tide are flowing in the same direction, the wavelength will be increased so that the gradient of the waves becomes less; the ride of a boat will be more comfortable because there will be more time between each wave crest for the boat to adapt to the changing shape of the wave.

When the wind and tide are flowing in opposite directions, the wavelength becomes shorter and the waves become steeper. In these conditions, the waves can be so short and steep that they are liable to break, and these wind against tide sea conditions are notable for the considerable increase in breaking waves. In conditions where the tide runs strongly, say above 2 to 3 knots, the wind against tide situation can produce quite severe sea conditions, which should be avoided if the wind is strong.

The sort of strong tidal conditions that can generate these short steep seas will usually be found in narrow channels and around headlands. Here the tidal streams tend to be more concentrated and these can also be the areas where the wind strength is likely to increase. The change in conditions from wind with tide to wind against tide can be quite dramatic and it can occur within an hour or two, so that it pays to be aware of this when on passage in coastal waters. You can experience the same effect when entering a narrow estuary or inlet.

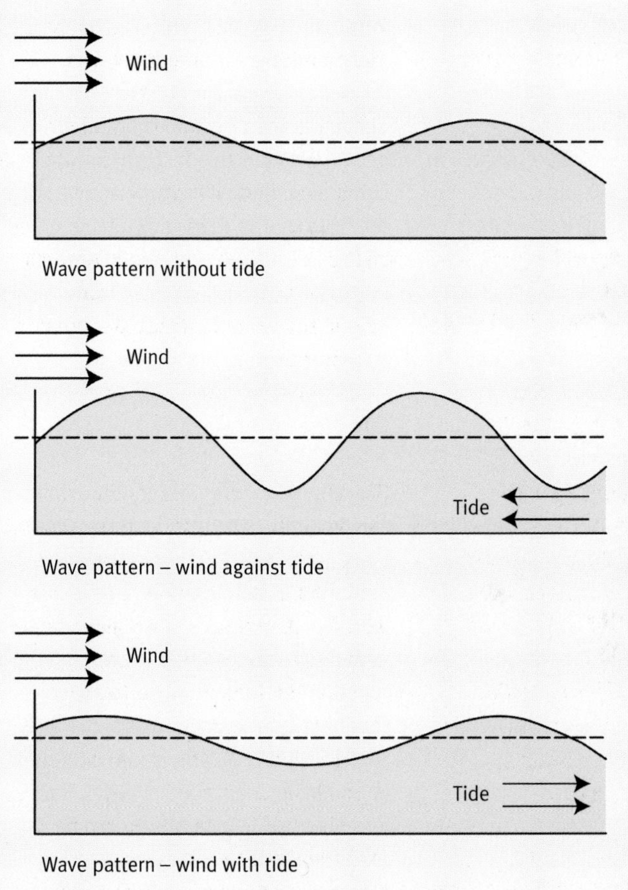

THE WAY IN WHICH THE WAVE PROFILE IS MODIFIED UNDER THE INFLUENCE OF CURRENTS OR TIDE.

26 WAVE REFRACTION

In open water, waves follow a fairly regular pattern, with the wave fronts all heading in roughly the same direction provided the wind has been blowing from the same direction for a while. This makes them easy to anticipate when you are driving a powerboat, but once the waves encounter shallow water or the land, things can be very different. Once the wave starts to 'feel' the bottom, then it is slowed down. When only a part of the wave is slowed in this way, but the main front moves on at the original speed, then the wave will appear to change direction or be refracted.

A wave front coming directly into the shore will encounter shallow water

WAVES REFRACTED AROUND A LARGE SHIP IN OPEN WATER.

along its whole length at the same time. This means that there will be no change in the direction of the wave front. It is when a wave encounters the shore at an angle that the direction change will occur, with the section in deep water continuing along its regular course while the inshore end slows down. This change in direction can produce some unexpected effects, causing what might appear to be sheltered waters to be come exposed to the sea.

One area where you'll find this type of refraction is around headlands, where the refracted waves will continue to sweep around the headland into what you might expect to be the sheltered side. This isn't going to be a particular worry unless you are looking for shelter or an anchorage on that lee side and you find that the seas there are bigger or rougher than expected. There can be a similar effect around a breakwater that is protecting a harbour, allowing the wave crests to enter what could be expected to be sheltered water.
More confused conditions can be found in the lee of an island, where the refracted waves will travel round each side of the island and then meet up again on the lee side. The two wave trains, one from each side and meeting on the lee side of the island, will be travelling in different directions when they meet. This means that they will in

effect be crossing wave trains, so that you could find an area of quite difficult sea conditions in the lee of the island, with steep pyramid waves created by the crossing waves.

You are likely to find this effect around small islands, but it might also be experienced around shoals where the same type of refraction can occur. Here the sea conditions could become more severe, because not only do you have the two refracted wave trains coming round the island but there will also be the waves that have passed over the top of the shoal. Again you're likely to find these conditions in the lee of isolated smaller shoals, but the resulting conditions can catch out the unwary because logic suggests that this is where you ought to find calmer conditions.

WAVES REFRACTED AROUND A HEADLAND, LEADING TO WAVES COMING INTO THE SUPPOSEDLY SHELTERED BAY.

27 WAVE HEIGHTS

The Beaufort Scale gives you some idea of the size of the waves associated with different wind strengths, but these figures are only a rough guide. Remember that the predicted wave heights given by the Scale are those that you might expect to find in open sea areas away from land, and you could find significant differences in inshore waters. At the bottom of the Beaufort Scale there is a warning to this effect: 'In enclosed waters or when near to land with an offshore wind, wave heights will be smaller and steeper.'

Obviously in the shelter of the land you'll almost certainly find smaller waves, because waves need a fetch (the distance upwind to the nearest land) of at least 320km (200 miles) to attain their expected height. You are unlikely to get this 320km fetch in inshore waters unless the coastline is fully exposed to the open sea. However, there are two other factors that can affect wave height, which come into play in inshore waters.

One factor is that the tidal current can affect the wave height and shape quite considerably. When the wind is against the tide, the wavelength is shortened as shown in Tides and waves, 25. This shortening of the wavelength will tend to increase the height of the wave and can produce quite difficult sea conditions.

The other factor that can affect wave height is shallow water. This effect can often be found in depths that are considerably greater than that required for safe navigation. A wave will start to 'feel' the bottom in depths that can be

A FORECAST CHART SHOWING THE ANTICIPATED HEIGHT AND DIRECTION OF THE WAVES.

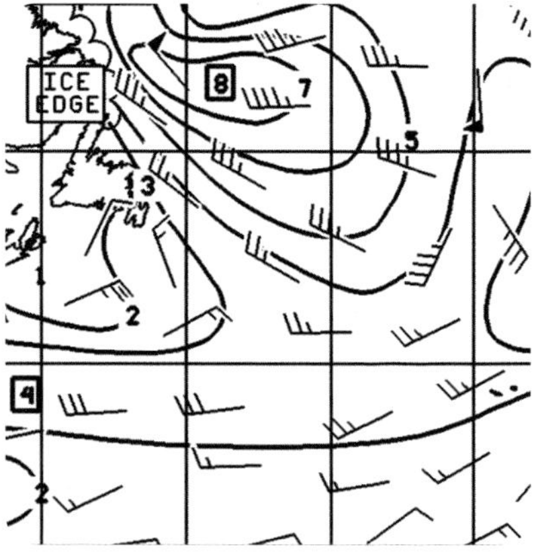

THE ASSOCIATED WIND FORECAST.

THE SORT OF SHORT STEEP WAVES YOU CAN FIND IN STRONG WINDS WHEN THE FETCH IS SHORT.

two or three times the wave height and there are suggestions that big ocean swells can be affected in water depths exceeding 100m (320ft). This 'feeling' of the sea bottom will slow the wave down, rather like the effect of an adverse tide, and in turn the wavelength will be shortened and its height increased.

In both these situations, the increase in wave height makes the wave more likely to break and there will be deterioration in the sea conditions, possibly making them dangerous. When trying to assess the possible sea conditions that you might experience in inshore waters, the critical factor is more likely to be the gradient of the wave than its actual height. As the gradient increases, the wavelength gets shorter and it becomes more difficult for a boat to negotiate the wave safely.

Some wave forecasts will give an indication of the wavelength to be expected; however, you won't find these forecasts for inshore waters because of the many variable factors that can affect waves, so you will need to make your own judgement, which means taking into account the wave height, tides, shallow water, topography of the land and the capability of the boat. Powerboats are more likely to be affected by steeper waves because of their higher speed potential.

28 THE EFFECT OF DEPTH ON SEA CONDITIONS

WAVES BREAKING IN THE SHALLOW WATERS AROUND A HEADLAND.

You only have to look at a beach to see how waves break when the water is really shallow - the waves are slowed and the gradient gets steeper. However, because of other factors there can be conditions where the depth of water is quite adequate for navigation but the relatively shallow water can still affect the sea conditions.

You probably see this to greatest effect in a harbour entrance where there is a bar. You know that there is adequate water in the entrance to get in but, from the way that the waves are breaking across the bar, there appears to be almost a physical barrier. Here, the waves become steeper and higher as they approach the shallow water – and this will become much more noticeable when the tide is on the ebb and the wind is against the tide. In these circumstances, you can encounter quite severe conditions that could make it dangerous to attempt to cross the bar to gain access to the harbour. Bear in mind that you may have the wind behind you as you approach the bar and, because the waves will then be breaking away from you, it may not be possible to get a picture of just how severe the conditions are.

To a lesser extent, you will see this same effect in many areas where there is a transition from deeper to shallower water. Once the wave starts to 'feel' the bottom, then it will start to become higher. In addition, the relative closeness of the seabed means that the wave is slowed down, and this also encourages it to grow higher and steeper. As it starts to get higher, the gradient increases and the wave can become unstable. This will normally happen when the gradient reaches 18 degrees.

Where the edge of a shoal shelves very gently, the effect may not be so noticeable compared with a steep-to shoal, where the sudden change in depth can lead to waves having a marked and considerable change in appearance, probably with breaking crests. Tides tend to be weaker over shoals except in harbour entrances, but obviously if the wind is against the tide, the change in wave appearance will be more noticeable (see Tides and waves, 25).

This change in the appearance of waves when they encounter shallow water can provide useful information. From a navigation point of view, the breaking waves will indicate a shoal area and that can help to establish your position or be a warning sign. The breaking crests also provide a warning that you could be entering an area of dangerous sea conditions. It is a time to take stock of where you are heading on both counts; and remember that one of the problems of navigating at night is that you're unlikely to be aware of the breaking waves until you actually encounter them.

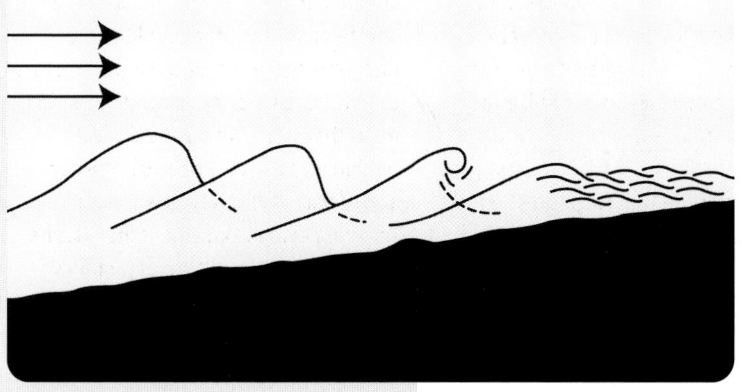

A BREAKING WAVE IN SHALLOW WATER. HERE THE WHOLE WAVE REARS UP AND BREAKS HEAVILY WITH CONSIDERABLE VIOLENCE

29 IDENTIFYING DANGEROUS SEA CONDITIONS

Several factors can contribute to dangerous conditions, apart from a strong wind, and if you identify these then you can often forecast where the bad conditions will be.

As we saw in The effect of depth on sea conditions, 28, shallow water will cause waves to break, so they are one factor to bear in mind. You will normally avoid these areas in your navigation planning; but, in strong winds, what might normally be safe navigation waters can start to create breaking waves and potential danger.

When the wind is against the tide, the waves become steeper and more prone to breaking. Strong tides can cause waves to break even when there is little wind but, in the main, dangerous conditions will only occur when a wind against tide situation is combined with one of the other factors.
The topography of the land can be one such factor. Around any pronounced headland the tidal flow is compressed and you can experience breaking waves, generated purely by this detour effect imposed on the water flow. You will find the same effect in narrow channels,

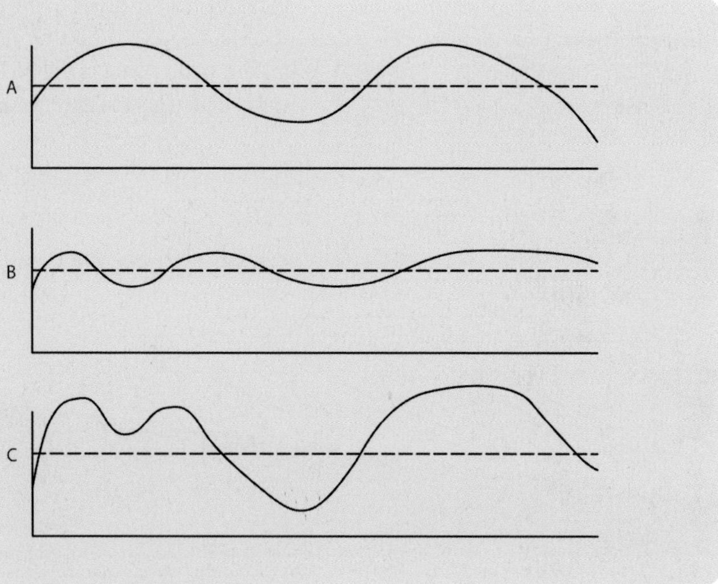

THE COMBINATION OF WAVE TRAINS A AND B PRODUCES THE WAVE PATTERN SHOWN IN C. THIS ACCOUNTS FOR THE IRREGULAR WAVE PATTERNS OFTEN FOUND AT SEA.

where the tidal flow will probably be accelerated as the channel narrows.

A strong tide running out of a harbour where there is a shallow water bar will create breaking waves. Any shoal that extends across the tide is quite likely to generate breaking waves with the up-swelling of the water, and in both of these situations the effect will be multiplied if there is a strong wind blowing against the tide. Around very pronounced headlands, you can even get a back eddy that curves around to flow back into the main channel. Where this back eddy and the main stream meet, there is likely to be a confused and possibly dangerous sea, even though this area may be located under the apparent lee of the headland.

So when you're trying to predict dangerous conditions, study the chart for areas where the tides are strong, where the water may be relatively shallow and where the topography of the land can interfere with the tidal flow. Add in a strong wind and it is not too hard to make predictions about the conditions that you might experience, although it will never be an exact science.

DANGEROUS SEA CONDITIONS CREATED BY A STRONG WIND MEETING A TIDE FLOWING IN THE OPPOSITE DIRECTION.

30 WHAT MAKES A WAVE BREAK

We have looked at some of the external causes of a breaking wave, but it will help you to forecast sea conditions and cope with breaking seas if you also understand the mechanism that prompts the wave to break.

The first thing to understand is that breaking waves in the open sea behave very differently to waves breaking on a shore or in very shallow water. It pays to watch waves in the open sea when the wind is strong. The first thing you'll notice is that a wave will tend to break in relatively isolated patches. Even a bigger than average wave won't have the long, breaking wave crest that you see on the beach, and only relatively small sections of the crest will break at any one time.

This partly emphasises the fact that waves tend to be quite irregular and along any wave front in the open sea there will be high and low areas. This is because there is very rarely just one set of waves out there. There may be a two- or three-wave train crossing, and where the crests of each wave meet there will be a peak, and where the crest of one meets the trough of another there will be a low.

Then watch the way the waves break. They rarely break with the type of big overhanging crest you see on the beach. Instead, just the top of the wave will start to run forward, and in doing so the crest will slow down and the main body of the wave will overtake the breaking crest. As a result, there isn't a big body of water moving forward in a breaking crest, which can be very dangerous – out in the open sea, the wave will rarely reach the critical 18-degree gradient that causes the wave to break fully. Rather, there are isolated patches of steep waves and these will break relatively harmlessly to restore the equilibrium in the wave.

Compare this with the solid body of breaking that moves forward onto a beach. Here the whole wave becomes unstable, partly because contact with the sea bottom is pushing the wave upwards and partly because the wave is being slowed and the gradient is increasing. The water will rear up and then crash forward. This is called a translation wave, and any such wave is very dangerous because there is a big release of energy as the wave breaks. You are only likely to experience this type of wave out in the open sea when there are very strong winds, and even then the breaking is likely to be patchy rather than continuous.

Finally, in understanding waves, it is worth repeating that a wave has to reach a gradient of 18 degrees before it becomes unstable and starts to break. This will help you to understand why the shortening of the wavelength when the wind is against the tide increases the gradient and causes more breaking waves. The pressure of the wind on the back of the wave also has an effect - the pressure tends to be higher nearer the top of the wave than at the bottom, where the wave is sheltered from the wind, and this promotes a breaking crest.

WAVES BREAKING HEAVILY IN SHALLOW WATER.

31 FETCH AND TIME

When forecasts give a wave height and other wave information, this is the height of the wave in open water away from any influence from the land or other factors. This information is relatively easy to calculate from research information, which is why it can be displayed with considerable confidence. For most boaters, who are operating in inshore waters, this information will only give a rough guide of what to expect out at sea, but you can get a better handle on the situation if you understand the influence of fetch and time.

Fetch is the distance upwind to the nearest land. This could only be a few miles if you're sailing in an estuary or it could be 160km (100 miles) in a sea area such as the English Channel. When the forecasters talk about wave sizes in open water, they will be considering the wave conditions when there is a fetch of at least 320km (200 miles). This is considered to be the distance necessary for waves to develop into the fully mature waves that are described in the forecast.

Anything less than this 320km distance and the waves are likely to have a reduced height – the lower diagram shows the effect on wave height of a reducing distance to the land upwind. If the fetch is reduced to 8km (5 miles) or less, then you should be in relatively sheltered waters where the waves won't seriously impede progress and comfort; but in very strong winds, even that 8km distance could produce quite nasty waves. We are talking here primarily about wave height, which of course is a significant factor, but the waves found in areas where the fetch is reduced are also likely to be steeper, which can make them more difficult to negotiate.

In Wave refraction, 26 we saw how the direction of travel of a wave train can be modified by land and shallow water. When we are considering the influence of fetch, it's useful to know that the effects of refraction are not likely to be felt immediately the fetch is reduced – for example, when you reduce it by passing behind a significant headland. Instead, there's likely to be a gradual reduction in wave size rather than a sudden change.

Time is the other factor involved in wave development and, even when the fetch is over 320km, it can take a considerable time from when the wind started to blow from that direction before the wave becomes fully mature. The upper diagram shows the sort of time lag that you might expect, but remember that these are only average figures and the weather doesn't always conform to averages. However, the diagram does indicate that there can be a margin of a few hours after a wind starts to blow hard before the waves get severe enough to impede progress, so there may be time to seek shelter before the waves mature.

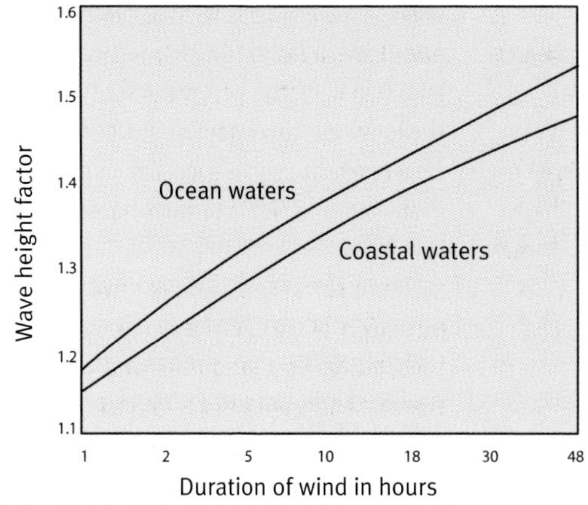

THE FACTORS BY WHICH WAVE HEIGHT CAN INCREASE WITH WIND DURATION IN OCEAN AND COASTAL WATERS.

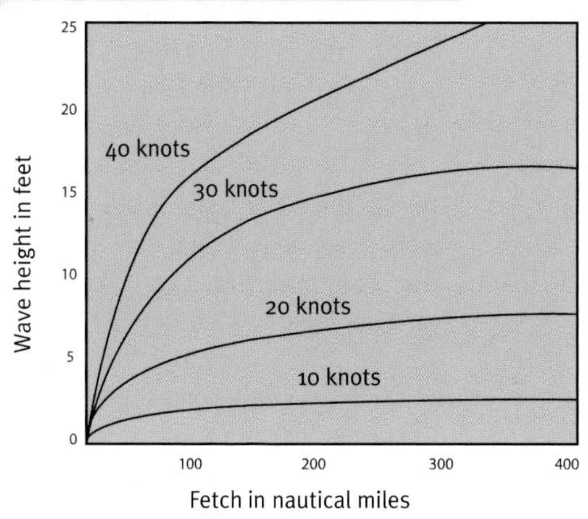

A GRAPH SHOWING THE WAY THAT WAVE HEIGHT INCREASES WITH FETCH IN VARIOUS WIND STRENGTHS

32 RADIATION FOG

Radiation fog is one of two types of fog that you're likely to come across at sea. It is a harbour fog rather than an open sea fog, and is the sort you will often find lying around when you wake up in the morning, giving you the impression that fog is going to prevent you from going to sea that day. By the time you have had breakfast and prepared for departure, however, you will often find that the radiation fog is clearing and you can head out after all.

To understand radiation fog, you need to know what causes it. The seeds for its development are usually sown overnight, when the land cools to the point where the water vapour in the air condenses into fog. This is why you'll only find this type of fog close to land, and why it tends to be most prevalent in harbours and on rivers – you could find that it is completely clear a kilometre or two out at sea. You will often find this fog developing in the very early morning, which is why you can wake up to find thick fog when you are in harbour.

Radiation fog is most likely to form over low-lying land and then drift out over the water as the water also cools. It also forms in hollows between higher land, which is why it can be found in harbours. It tends to be more prevalent in autumn and winter when the air holds more moisture and the nights are longer so there is more time for cooling down. The other requirement for radiation fog

RADIATION FOG IS MOST PREVALENT IN HARBOURS AND ON RIVERS.

RADIATION FOG STARTING TO LIFT AS THE SUN BURNS IT OFF.

to form is that the air is still. If there is any wind then there will be a greater mixing of the air, and the temperature differences required for the formation of radiation fog are less likely to occur. Radiation fog is only likely to form near to the land where this temperature difference exists, and if you can navigate through the fog to the sea you will often find clear conditions.

Another thing to know about radiation fog is that it will only exist close to the surface of the water, sometimes no more than 10m (33ft) above the surface. This means that, in theory, you could climb the mast of a sailboat and get a clear view - but of course you will only see anything tall enough to stick up clear of the fog. You should be able to see ships, but you will not pick up the vital buoys and small craft that you need to see in order to navigate safely.

Although mainly found in harbours, you can encounter radiation fog anywhere along the coast, and you may see it when you approach from seaward in the form of layers of fog against the land. That should act as a warning sign that you might soon enter a fog bank as you close the land.

33 ADVECTION FOG

In contrast to radiation fog, advection fog is the type that you are likely to find out at sea, and it can extend for considerable areas over the water. The basic cause of advection fog is when warm, moist air flows over colder water or land. When the warm, moist air meets with the colder surface, the temperature of the air that is in close contact with the water is reduced, and this causes some of the moisture in the air to condense out and form the fog.

It is not always easy to identify the conditions in which this type of fog might occur because the forecasts do not normally include the necessary temperature and humidity information. However, you can get a guide if you see that the forecast winds are coming in from a warm direction from the sea and are likely to meet areas of colder water inshore. The conditions for this sort of fog to form can be quite critical and it may take only a few degrees' change in temperature to dictate whether or not the fog will form - hence the difficulty of forecasting advection fog precisely.

ADVECTION FOG IN COASTAL WATERS.

Areas that might possibly be affected by this type of fog could be identified if you have sufficiently detailed sea temperature charts, and these are now becoming a feature of more detailed forecasts. These could show areas of colder water, and if the wind is blowing in from warmer, open sea areas where the air can pick up moisture, then fog could result. The limits of this type of fog are not clearly defined and fog forecasts are usually general in nature rather than specific. Advection fog can occur at any time of the year but will obviously be more prevalent when the required temperature differences occur – in European waters, this is likely to be in the latter half of the year as the land and near-sea temperatures start to fall.
One of the causes of advection fog can be a cold-water current meeting a warmer wind. This is found on the East Coast of Canada and the United States, where the cold Labrador Current flowing south from the Arctic generates fog when it meets the warm moist air flowing north with the Gulf Stream. There can be fog 50 per cent of the time in areas off the east coast of the US and Canada as a result of this, extending over the spring and summer months.

In the English Channel, warm air flowing in from the Atlantic on a south-westerly wind can meet the colder water of the Channel and create fog, particularly in the autumn. On a smaller scale, colder water inshore meeting warmer, moister air coming in from seaward can be responsible for coastal fogs, which tend to be known simply as sea fogs. In all cases of advection fog, it is likely to be changes in the wind direction or strength that will cause the fog to clear.

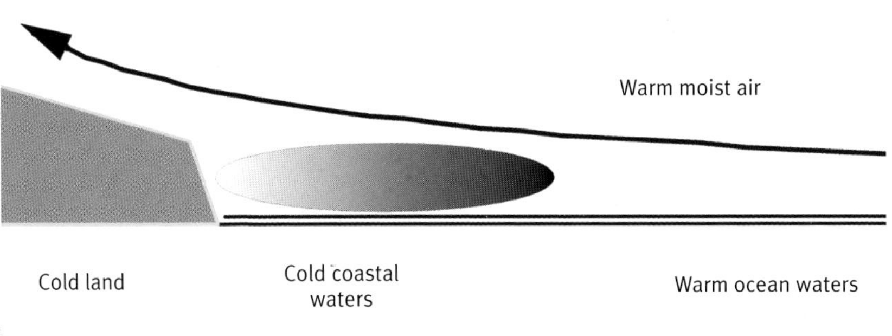

THE WAY IN WHICH ADVECTION FOG CAN BE FORMED WHEN WARM MOIST AIR MEETS COLDER WATERS INSHORE.

34 WHEN WILL THE FOG CLEAR?

RADIATION FOG STARTING TO LIFT.

When you are in fog, the one thing you want to know is when it will clear. Having some idea about the time the fog is likely to lift will enable you to plan a strategy to cope – but forecasting fog and when it will clear is notoriously difficult. Even when the general conditions may be changing, fog can still persist in local pockets where those changes have not occurred or are delayed. Knowing when the fog might clear can be particularly important when you are at sea and trying to make a landfall; but it can also be important when you are in harbour waiting for the fog to clear so that you can head out.

The time scale will depend a great deal on the type of fog you are dealing with, and Radiation fog, 32 and Advection fog, 33 should help with identification. In harbour, when you are waiting to sail in the morning, it will almost certainly be radiation fog that you encounter, and that is likely to clear when the sun becomes strong enough to 'burn' off the fog and restore some sort of temperature equilibrium. In normal circumstances, this will occur by mid-morning – but there are no guarantees, and radiation fog can persist all day, particularly if there is a layer of cloud above the fog that stops the temperatures from rising. There can be days, usually in the autumn or winter, when a radiation fog will last all day. This can occur when the sun isn't strong enough to make an appreciable change in the land temperatures and when conditions remain still.

Radiation fog will also normally disappear if a breeze springs up to blow it away, but again it can require a temperature difference for the breeze to develop. If the forecast is suggesting wind, then you can expect a clearance when the wind comes along. Radiation fog does not normally extend far out to sea and you may be able to get an idea of conditions at sea by listening or talking to craft already out there. If you know it is clear, you may want to navigate the fog over the short distance to the open sea.

Fog at sea is most likely to be advection fog when a warm, moist wind is blowing over a cooler sea. While these conditions persist, the fog is likely to remain, but a change in wind direction or possibly strength could see the fog clearing. The forecast should indicate when such a wind shift is likely to occur to help with the fog prediction, but you could also see a clearance if you are moving into warmer waters (although that is more difficult to forecast).

Predicting the clearance of fog is never a precise science and the timing is not easy to forecast. Local changes in conditions such as those described are likely to be your best indication, but they aren't likely to give a great deal of warning before the fog actually clears. Even when you get a clearance, it may only be temporary, and other craft could be in a fog bank close by where you cannot see them.

TYPE OF FOG AND SEASON	AREAS AFFECTED AT THE FRONT	FACTORS FOR FORMATION	FACTORS FOR DISPERSAL
RADIATION FOG (usually October to March)	Inland and harbour areas particularly where the surrounding land is low lying and moist	Cooling due to radiation from the ground on clear nights when the wind is light - usually a feature of anti-cyclone weather	Dispersed when the sun's heat warms the ground or by an increase in the wind strength
ADVECTION FOG (Usually spring and early summer when seas are still cool)	Sea and adjacent coasts and may penetrate into harbours. Also open seas where cold waters exist	Cooling of warmer moist air when it comes into contact with the cooler seas	Usually disperses when the wind direction changes and it can also be dispersed near coasts when the sun warms the land/sea
FRONTAL FOG (At all seasons)	Mainly over high ground and occasionally at sea	Lowering of the cloud base along the line of a frontal system	Dispersed when the front passes through

35 DRIZZLE

Drizzle is one of the more depressing weather phenomena at sea. Not only does it reduce visibility, sometimes to near fog limits, and reduce the effectiveness of radar at the same time, but it is usually associated with little or no wind, which can be bad news for sailboats.

Drizzle is usually associated with 'occlusions', those frontal systems that are formed when a depression is mature and the cold front has merged with the warm front. This happens because a cold front will tend to move faster than a warm front, so the catching-up process starts close to the centre of the depression and gradually moves outwards. When this happens, the weather associated with the two fronts becomes less active, resulting in lighter winds and less intense rainfall.

In an occluded front, the cold air ahead of the warm front and the cold air of the cold front join together at sea level and this forces the remnants of the warm air between the two cold areas to rise. In rising, the warm air wants to shed what moisture is remaining and this is what falls in the form of light rain or drizzle.

The weather associated with the drizzle may vary considerably from low heavy clouds when the warm air is still quite low to higher clouds, although in the latter case the drizzle will prevent you from seeing the clouds anyway.

An occluded front can have a long extended tail that curves around the low as it matures, and this tail will often be found to be running from east to west. With the weather patterns generally running from west to east, this means that you could find yourself in the extended occlusion tail for a considerable period, and the drizzle and its associated weak winds could last for many hours. Although the conditions are relatively benign, the weather is depressing and is made more so by its reluctance to change.

Another situation where drizzle can be found is when a warm front has just passed and you are in the warm sector that follows. This is also an area where the weather can be less active, particularly if the fronts are weak, and here you may find showers or drizzle. The advent of drizzle is most likely when you are in a coastal area where the land faces the wind.

The difference in the conditions required to form rain or drizzle can be quite small, so it can be fairly difficult to forecast just when drizzle will occur rather than rain, but drizzle is more likely when the frontal systems are mild and relatively inactive. As far as the effect is concerned, you will find a considerable reduction in visibility in drizzle, as well as a noticeable absence of wind, and the conditions can persist for quite a time, even up to 24 hours.

DRIZZLE CAN CAUSE MISERABLE CONDITIONS AT SEA, REDUCING THE VISIBILITY CONSIDERABLY.

36 GUSTS

The atmosphere is pretty turbulent and this turbulence occurs at several levels of scale. On global scale, there are the high and low pressure areas with the wind circulating round them, and then there are more local areas of turbulence, such as those associated with frontal systems. On a very local scale, there are gusts of wind that may exist over an area of only a few hundred metres. While these gusts may not be particularly significant in the greater scheme of things, they can present a difficult situation for small craft, particularly sailboats.

Gusts are generally short-lived, but because the wind speed can temporarily double in speed over a local area they can pose a significant danger to sailboats. Powerboats will be less affected because the increased wind in the gusts rarely lasts for more than a few minutes, and this doesn't give time for the sea conditions to change appreciably. You can sometimes be made aware of gusts approaching by the local disturbance on the surface of the sea, but you're only likely to see this in relatively calm conditions, such as inside a harbour. Out at sea, the disturbance of the sea surface is likely to be lost in the general surface disturbance of the waves, although you may see spray being blown off the top of the wave because of the increased wind strength.

Gusts are obviously going to be more prevalent close to shore, where the flow of the wind will be more uneven owing to the interference from the land. Out in the open sea, gusts are caused mainly by the interaction between the wind and the sea surface. Close to the surface, the friction between the airflow and the sea will slow the wind down to a degree, but

WIND SPEED RANGE	FACTOR FOR MAXIMUM GUST SPEED	FACTOR FOR MEAN GUST SPEED
Daytime		
Force 3 – 4	2.0	1.6
Force 4 – 5	1.8	1.5
Force 5 – 6	1.6	1.4
Night-time		
Force 3 – 4	1.9	1.5
Force 4 – 5	1.8	1.4
Force 5 – 6	1.7	1.4

this slowing is likely to be uneven and it is the uneven airflow that can generate wind gusts.

The increase of the wind strength within a gust can be quite considerable, as the table shows, and it tends to vary with the wind strength. With a force 3 wind the strength can double in a gust, but when you get to force 5 winds the increase is more modest. However, remember that a force 5 wind covers a greater range of wind strengths than the winds lower down the scale, so a gust can make a significant different to the conditions. The strength of gusts also decreases at night, which is a blessing, as you'll get little or no indication of the arrival of a gust in the dark.

Because gusts tend to be spontaneous and will materialise with little or no warning, the arrival of a gust means that you'll have little time to respond to the increase in wind speed. This is one of the reasons why it is good practice to avoid carrying excessive sail for the average wind conditions you are experiencing.

LOOK FOR GUSTS UNDERNEATH THE CLOUDS IN THIS ACTIVE LOOKING SKY.

37 SQUALLS

Squalls are different from gusts in that they are more predicable, at least in the short term, and you're likely to get some warning of their arrival in daylight, although night-time detection can present problems. Squalls will be found where two airflows mix or where there is a rising airflow owing to warming or similar disturbances. You will almost certainly find squalls along a cold front because of the intensity of the front and the mixing of the air masses. Along a cold front the squalls can merge together into line squalls (see Line squalls and waterspouts, 40). Squalls are less likely along a warm front, where the mixing of the airflows is less intense, and there is very little chance of finding squalls in an occluded front where conditions tend to be less active.

Squalls of a milder form can be found under areas of cloud where the cloud indicates that there is a mixing of air as warmer air rises. Here, the wind increase in the squall is likely to be moderate owing to the less intense nature of the activity, but such a temporary increase in wind strength can be useful for sailboats if you can detect it on a day of light winds. This type of squall will be found mostly in the summer when the local heating can be more intense.

Squalls can often be found near land when the wind is stronger, particularly if the wind is off the land or along the coastline and the land is fairly high. In this situation, it is the land that interferes with the flow of air and creates eddies in the flow that can develop into squalls.

A squall can last up to an hour but is more likely to be of shorter duration, often no more than 15 minutes. The cloud activity is likely to be your early warning sign of an approaching squall, and you can expect to experience quite sharp squalls when you see intense cloud activity. Severe squalls often occur in thunderstorms and even without this type of intense activity a squall will often be accompanied by rain, which will help you to identify its presence from a distance. You can even track the progress of a squall if it is associated with rain, which can be useful if you feel the need to take avoiding action.

At night the detection of squalls can be difficult. There will be little in the way of any visual indication until the squall hits you, although if there is rain associated with the squall it should be possible to pick it up on radar.

Like gusts, squalls are mainly a problem for sailboats and can call for a shortening of sail for the duration of the squall. Longer duration squalls can lead to an increase in the size of waves and this can cause problems for smaller powerboats, particularly if the wind in the squall is against the flow of the tide.

Also be aware that there can be a temporary change in wind direction as the squall passes through.

AN APPROACHING RAIN SQUALL THAT IS ALSO LIKELY TO BRING AN INCREASE IN WIND STRENGTH.

EXPECT SQUALLS UNDER BLACK CLOUDS LIKE THESE.

38 THUNDERSTORMS

We tend to think of thunderstorms as just bringing heavy rain and reduced visibility for a while, perhaps associated with some spectacular lightning displays. However, don't underestimate thunderstorms, as they can represent one of the more violent forms of local weather. For sailboats they can produce some quite violent local winds, and while these aren't likely to last long enough to generate any serious change in sea conditions, the heavy rain found in thunderstorms can be a short-term problem for boats of all types.

The type of thunderstorms that form out at sea are usually associated with a very active cold front. This is particularly the case when the temperature difference between the warm and colder air masses is considerable, as often occurs in a very active frontal system. Such an active front can sometimes be recognised by the considerable wind shift that occurs in the front, which alone could be enough to start the process of a thunderstorm forming. Combine this wind shift with the temperature differences associated with the front and you have the very active conditions that can trigger thunderstorms.

In daylight you should be able to recognise thunderstorms from quite a distance – they are easily recognised by the anvil cloud when they are fully formed, and the very dark base cloud can be another indicator. At night, the lightning will reveal their presence, but this can be visible over quite a large part of the sky and it isn't always easy to pinpoint just where the thunderstorm is located.

DON'T UNDERESTIMATE THUNDERSTORMS.

39 AVOIDING THUNDERSTORMS

Thunderstorms are best avoided if the navigation situation allows you to vary the course, and the avoidance tactics are very similar to those you might use to avoid collision with other craft – except that it would be sensible to allow the thunderstorm the right of way.

If your craft is fitted with radar, a thunderstorm will show up as quite a distinctive target. The heavy rain creates a large and usually quite sharp-edged target that can be quite irregular in shape and will be considerably larger than any ship target, so you are unlikely to mistake it for anything else.

If you put the bearing cursor on the centre of the thunderstorm target on the radar, you know you will pass clear if the thunderstorm return moves away from the bearing cursor. There should be a significant movement of the target in relation to the bearing cursor if you plan to pass well clear; if the bearing of the thunderstorm target remains steady or only changes slightly in relation to the bearing cursor over a period of a few minutes, it could be time to make an alteration of course by, say, 30 degrees or more to clear the thunderstorm.

Without radar, you can still employ the compass bearing techniques used for ship collision avoidance. With a visual sighting of the thunderstorm, take a compass bearing, and if this changes significantly over a period of a few minutes the thunderstorm should pass clear. If the compass bearing doesn't change, it is time to take avoiding action.

At night you will still see the thunderstorm on the radar, so the same avoidance technique can be used, but you could find it difficult to pinpoint the location of the storm accurately enough to use compass bearings.

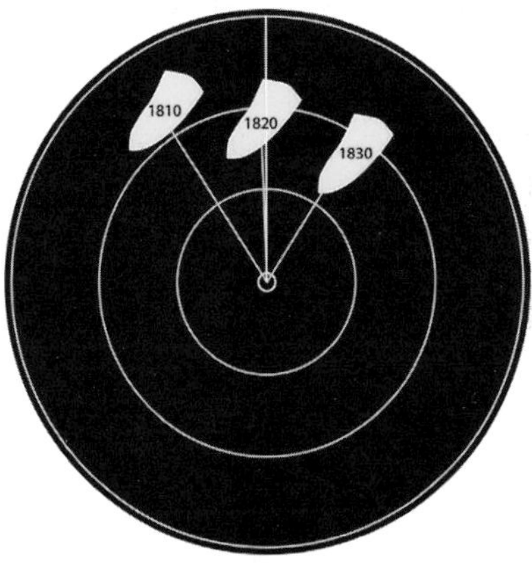

THUNDERSTORMS AND HEAVY SHOWERS SHOW UP WELL ON THE RADAR AND THE RADAR CAN BE USED TO PLOT AVOIDING ACTION. THE TECHNIQUE OF PUTTING THE BEARING CURSOR ON THE TARGET WILL SHOW HOW IT IS MOVING AND IN THIS CASE AN ALTERATION TO PORT WOULD BE THE BEST AVOIDING ACTION.

40 LINE SQUALLS AND WATERSPOUTS

Line squalls tend to be associated with tropical waters, although they can occur in moderate climates. They are recognisable by the hard line of dark cloud that can sometimes stretch from horizon to horizon and looks very threatening as it comes closer. There is something about the appearance of a line squall that instils fear, and it is well to heed this instinct because a line squall can contain some severe weather. You can encounter a similar type of threatening line cloud as a cold front passes through, but the true line squall will normally feature very dark clouds at its base and stretch further than its cold front equivalent.

Although the true line squall appears to be longer than the type of line clouds associated with cold fronts, they are in fact a relatively local phenomenon, whereas a cold front can stretch for hundreds of kilometres. You can find line squalls as part of a cold front, however, although they won't extend for the length of the front and will be focused on areas of more severe disturbance. So the line squall is a relatively local weather disturbance rather than a more general one, and won't normally appear in a weather forecast. It's usually a difference in heating and cooling of air masses that produces line squalls, something like a thunderstorm but in a line rather than in a single focused point.

In terms of effect, a line squall can produce some quite devastating weather. Look for violent squalls as the line squall passes through, and there can also be very heavy rain, sometimes in patches and sometimes along the length of the squall. Line squalls are also the main breeding ground for waterspouts.

Waterspouts are considered to be mainly a tropical phenomenon, but they do occur in more northern waters such as the English Channel as well as in the Mediterranean. A waterspout is the marine equivalent of a tornado, a compact mass of air swirling at a very high speed. They are easily recognised, even though their length, diameter and shape can vary, and it isn't easy to determine their course.

You should avoid waterspouts at all costs as they can be very damaging to small craft. You can use the same techniques as shown for avoiding thunderstorms, but you're likely to have less time available to take avoiding action. Also watch out for multiple waterspouts, and in the tropics you can often see a line of waterspouts descending from the same line cloud. Although they tend to be short-lived, sailboats should drop all sail and motor away, while power craft are best advised to turn and run away as fast as possible, navigation circumstances permitting.

AN INTENSE LINE SQUALL THAT MIGHT GENERATE WATERSPOUTS.

A YACHT ABOUT TO ENCOUNTER A LINE SQUALL.

A WATERSPOUT BELOW A LINE SQUALL.

41 THE MESSAGE FROM THE CLOUDS

FAIR WEATHER CUMULUS CLOUDS.

DRAMATIC CLOUDS LIKE THIS WILL INDICATE SOME FAIRLY INTENSE WEATHER CONDITIONS.

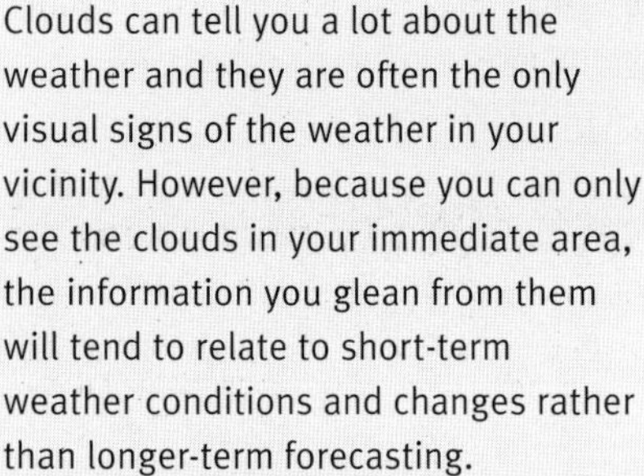

Clouds can tell you a lot about the weather and they are often the only visual signs of the weather in your vicinity. However, because you can only see the clouds in your immediate area, the information you glean from them will tend to relate to short-term weather conditions and changes rather than longer-term forecasting.

Some cloud forms are very easy to identify and have a clear meaning. Thunderstorm clouds have a very distinctive form (see Thunderstorms, 38) and the high Cirrus associated with an on-coming warm front is covered in Clouds in a warm front, 42. Isolated clouds can indicate the presence of a local area of stronger winds and, as a general rule, the lower the cloud, the greater the chance of rain associated with it. However, you also need to look for some of the more subtle signs from the clouds to obtain an indication of what is going on in the short term.
Out at sea you may frequently see a darker-looking cloud, often with a fairly straight base, in an otherwise gentle-looking sky. This may not herald rain, particularly if you cannot see the grey rain below the cloud, but it could certainly indicate a local wind disturbance below that cloud. The cloud itself is formed by the intermixing of local airstreams that have been disturbed by heating or eddies, and this generally means that there will be gusts or even modest squalls below the cloud.

Some clouds, usually of the Cumulus or Cumulonimbus types, will look active with their towering billowy structure, and you can be fairly sure of considerable wind activity below such clouds. When these clouds have a diffused or wispy edge, they are probably even more active – and active clouds mean active weather.
The speed at which the clouds are travelling also gives an indication of wind strength. Low clouds rushing across the sky will indicate wind, but you will probably already be aware of that. It is often the higher clouds that can give more information for the future, and if you are able to see the very high cirrus cloud moving, you

know that the jet stream way up in the sky is strong and active, which almost certainly means strong winds to come.

In the past, clouds were one of the very few weather indicators available to forecasters, and they could read a lot into what the clouds were doing; but the accuracy levels of any forecast based on the clouds will not be good except in the very short term. Today, with sophisticated computer forecasting and satellite images, cloud messages tend to get ignored. Nevertheless, it is the clouds that give you the 'feel' for the weather, and they can help to make the forecast for your area more specific.

CLOUD NAMES

NAME OF CLOUD AND USUAL ABBREVIATION	RANGE OF HEIGHT OF CLOUD IN METRES	VERTICAL THICKNESS OF CLOUD MASS	SIGNIFICANT FEATURES
Cirrus (Ci)	6,000 to 12,000	Generally a few hundred metres	Usually indicates and approaching frontal system
Cirrostratus (Cs)	6,000 to 12,000	Generally a few hundred metres	Usually indicates an approaching frontal system – sometimes with haloes around the sun
Cirrocmmulus (Cc)	6,000 to 12,000	Fairly thin	–
Altocummulus (Ac)	2,000 to 6,000	A few hundred metres	Bands are often seen ahead of fronts
Altostratus (As)	2,000 to 6,000	Up to 3,500 metres	Indicates closeness of the rain area of a front
Nimbostratus(Ns)	100 to 600	Up to 4,500 metres	Associated with precipitation
Stratus (St)	150 to 600	From 30 to 300 metres	May cover high ground as fog
Stratocummulus (Sc)	300 to 1,400	From 150 to 900 metres	–
Cummulus (Cu)	600 to 1,400	From 1,400 to 4,500 metres	Usually indicates a more stable weather pattern
Cummulonimbus (Cb)	600 to 1,400	From 300 to 9,000 metres	Very turbulent cloud usually with heavy showers and often thunder and lightening

42 CLOUDS IN A WARM FRONT

A warm front is where warm air is moving in over colder air, and is a significant weather feature. As the warm air meets the colder air, it rises, with the meeting line between the two air masses following an angled path up and over the cold air – and this creates a very distinctive cloud sequence. Knowing the sequence, and being able to recognise where you are in that sequence, will enable you to get an indication of the progress of the front and allow you to estimate when it might pass through, with the consequent wind change that follows.

The cloud sequence in a warm front is like a rolling display of most of the main cloud types, the type of cloud changing and getting lower until the point where the warm air is found at sea level and the cold air has passed by. The first cloud to indicate the approaching front will be the very high streaks of Cirrus. If these appear to be hooked or turned up at the end, look for a more active front.

The Cirrus will quite quickly become obscured, first by heavier Altocumulus cloud and then by darker Altostratus, the clouds getting steadily thicker and lower. As the cloud ceiling lowers further, and the cloud turns to Stratus and then Nimbostratus, the rain is likely to start and you may no longer be able to determine cloud types; but at this stage you know that the end of the frontal area isn't far away, and the rain section is unlikely to last for more than four hours, assuming that the front is passing across at normal speed. You may find the cloud changes are prolonged if the front is angled in relation to the course of the depression with which it is associated.

The cloud forms in a warm front may be anywhere between 150km and 800km (100 and 500 miles), and only the rate of change of the cloud formations will give an indication; however, you may not know the angle at which the front is passing, so distance isn't a clear guide for timing. Fronts also move at different speeds, usually anywhere between 10 and 40 knots. Two consecutive weather charts can give an indication of the speed and direction of travel of a warm front, but you know that when the rain starts there is likely to be between 150km and 300km (100 and 200) miles of rain, which could take several hours to pass.

When the rain stops, you know that the front has passed through and the heavy low clouds will be replaced, probably by Cumulus clouds, but the change will be quite slow. Warm fronts do not generally have the clear-cut changes associated with cold fronts and, as the front passes through, the first sign of change may be just a lifting of the cloud ceiling, even before the rain has stopped.

CLOUDS IN A WARM FRONT

HIGH HOOKED CIRRUS CLOUD THAT CAN HERALD AN ADVANCING WARM FRONT.

43 DEEPENING DEPRESSIONS

When a deepening depression is forecast, you can assume that the weather will get worse. Not only does a deepening depression mean that the isobars are likely to be closer together, which will mean stronger winds, but it generally means that the rate of travel of the weather system will speed up. As a general rule, the deeper the depression, the faster it will travel. If it's travelling in your direction, then it is time to consider your tactics quickly and take action.

If you are in harbour, it could be sensible to abandon going to sea until you have a clearer idea of what the weather is going to do. It certainly doesn't make sense to go to sea on a worsening forecast unless you only have to make a short passage and think you can complete it before the blow comes in. A depression that is getting deeper is almost certainly a precursor to worsening weather and its arrival is a time for caution.

If you are at sea, then you need to consider your options carefully. Much will depend on the distance to the depression and how extensive its weather system is. In this situation, you'll want the most accurate weather information you can get to enable you to make a valid judgement about tactics. Ideally, you want to be able to predict when the severe weather might reach your particular location so you can gauge how much time you have remaining to escape the storm. You should evaluate the distance to the nearest good shelter – preferably in a good sheltered harbour rather than behind a headland, because in the longer term the wind direction may change and render your shelter useless, leaving you exposed.

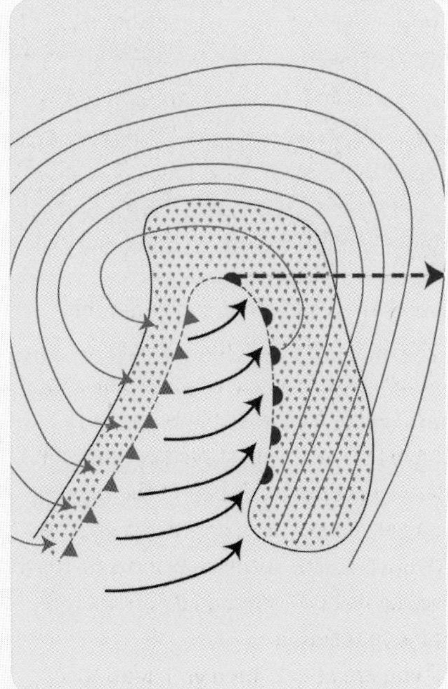

A TYPICAL NORTHERN HEMISPHERE DEPRESSION WITH SHADED SECTION SHOWING THE MAIN RAIN AREAS AND THE BROKEN ARROW SHOWING THE DIRECTION OF TRAVEL. THE STRONGER ARROWS DENOTE THE WARM AIR SECTION OF THE DEPRESSION.

Getting the clear, accurate weather information that you need in this situation when you are at sea isn't always easy, and this will be the time you wish you had invested in an Internet connection on board! However, if you have been at sea for a while you should have gained a good indication of the weather patterns, and if you combine this with the barometer readings and the verbal weather forecasts you should be able to sharpen your timing.

If shelter doesn't look to be a viable option before the storm arrives, then set a course that should take you away from the worst effects of the pending storm. There are no hard and fast rules here because there can be so many variables to consider, but the aim should be to reduce your exposure to the strong winds in terms of time. The important thing is to recognise a worsening situation as early as possible so that you have the maximum time in which to take avoiding action. Waiting for the weather to change before you take action is not a viable option. Time can be the most valuable commodity you have when dealing with bad weather.

44 SECONDARY LOWS

In an ideal world, the weather would consistently follow a steady pattern, with a series of high and low pressure areas sweeping across higher latitudes. That is certainly the main general pattern and it can be forecast for several days ahead with considerable accuracy. The trouble is that there are often small irregularities in this general pattern and these can develop at quite short notice to upset the longer-term forecast.

If you spend some time studying weather maps, you will notice that while the main low-pressure areas tend to run along a well-forecast course from west to east most of the time, some new low-pressure areas can develop quite rapidly. These secondary lows are extra to the main forecast and because they tend to develop at relatively short notice, they can bring worsening weather at the same short notice. They can also follow a different path than the main low-pressure areas and often seem to want to join up with the main low.

These secondary lows are like the eddies that you see in a stream of water and they can develop along a cold front where the secondary low starts off as an eddy in the main airflow around the primary low. Provided it is supplied with energy in the form of heat, perhaps from a warmer sea or over land, it can develop into quite a vigorous compact low-pressure area with associated strong winds. Because of this requirement for heat energy, these secondary lows tend to form to the south (north in the Southern hemisphere) of the main depression. Normally they will want to head north to join the main low-pressure area, but there is no guarantee of this.

Because these secondary lows are developing within the main airflow, the wind patterns that develop around them have to fit into the general wind flow. This can lead to a tightening of the isobars in the local area around the secondary low as it tries to squeeze in, resulting in some local areas of quite strong winds. It brings a fluidity to the more stable weather situation and can cause short-term changes.

The main problem with these secondary lows is that they are difficult to forecast except at short notice and thus it can be equally difficult to work out tactics to deal with the change. As a general rule, when you want to avoid a vigorous developing secondary low where good shelter is not readily available, head to the south (north in the Southern hemisphere) because the secondary low will normally head north.

A lot will depend on the relative positions of the main and secondary lows and your position in relation to them. One thing is for sure though, you need to treat these secondaries with great respect because they can be both quite violent and fast-moving and the forecasts, which are generally run only every 12 hours, can have difficulty in keeping up with them.

FORCE 10 NORTH ATLANTIC.

45 USING SATELLITE INFORMATION

Pictures from satellites have become a new tool for forecasters and more recently it has been possible for yachtsmen to download their own satellite pictures. These can give you the view from 300km (200 miles) above of what the weather is doing on the surface of the earth; but while they can be a valuable tool for forecasting, these satellite pictures do have limitations.

The biggest limitation of any satellite picture is that, while the picture will show the swirling clouds of a low-pressure area and measure the progress of the weather, this is all historical information. The satellite pictures are not forecasts – they only show what is going on at the present time. A satellite picture is reporting on the current weather and, to a forecaster, this can be valuable information for predicting the future; but for the yachtsman out at sea, you already know to a certain extent what the current weather is, because you are experiencing it. So for all their good looks and wonderful technology, satellite pictures do not present an eye into the future.

Their main value lies in enabling you to see the extent of the weather. A variety of formats can be produced by satellite pictures, but the ones that are of most interest will be those pictures taken using visible light. These will show the extent of the cloud cover and that can be a good indication of what is going on below. By knowing your own position on the satellite picture, you can see where you are in relation to the moving weather, and this should enable you to get a better idea of when to expect changes.

You could, for example, see the typical cloud cover of a warm front that is lying out to the west of your position. From this, you should be able to estimate when you will start seeing the first signs of the front arriving. Alternatively, if you're in the frontal zone already then you should be able to get some idea of how long the frontal conditions will last, and when you can expect the usual frontal wind shift to occur.

Satellite pictures can be more valuable when you have two successive pictures, perhaps taken a few hours apart. From these, you will be able to see the speed of travel of the weather features, and by using these in conjunction with any weather maps you should have a better indication of the weather conditions.

Sophisticated software can take successive satellite pictures and transform them into a moving picture of the weather, like those you see on TV – these can give a better picture of what is going on, but remember that you are watching history.

Satellite pictures are available in different formats. The usual one is taken with visible light, but this won't work at night. The main alternative is infrared pictures that can show varying temperatures, but these need more expert interpretation. On visible light pictures, it's often possible to see fog patches – as long as there is no cloud above the fog – and this enables you to see the extent of the fog.

Satellite pictures are generally only available over the Internet, and it won't always be possible to get them at sea, so in the main satellite pictures are for study before you go to sea.

SATELLITE PICTURES LOOK VERY IMPRESSIVE BUT THEY CAN ONLY SHOW THE CURRENT AND HISTORICAL WEATHER PATTERNS.

46 RUNNING FOR SHELTER

When you find yourself out at sea with a deteriorating weather forecast and you are thinking about running for shelter, you need to consider seriously what your options are. So much will depend on the prevailing situation, and what in the short term looks like the obvious solution might not turn out to be the right choice in the long term. Timing is a vital element in any decision to seek shelter and the earlier you make the decision, the better chance you have of a successful outcome.

The temptation is always going to be to turn and run away from the wind and weather. Running downwind will not only give the impression of running away from the storm, but there will also be the feeling of higher speeds and better progress combined with a more comfortable ride, particularly in a powerboat.

Running downwind can be a viable option if there is good shelter located at some point on the route. The problem that may arise, and which you should consider, is that any harbour downwind is going to be exposed to the full force of the wind that is blowing from behind you. If there is any shallow water in the entrance or a bar across the entrance, you could find yourself heading into difficult or even dangerous conditions when you reach the harbour.

Before making any decisions, you need to look at all the options. Heading upwind is going to seem like a very unpleasant option, but if there is land up to windward then it could prove to be the best solution. As you close the land you are going to come in under its shelter, so the conditions should improve the further you travel. There may be some short-term pain but there will be longer-term gain as you reach the shelter of the land.

In making any decision about seeking shelter, you need to consider various factors. Firstly, you need the best weather information available so that your decision is based on valid data. Then there are the meteorological factors to consider, such as any expected changes in wind strength and direction – the expected timing of these changes can be vital to your planning. In a planing powerboat, you may have the speed potential to outrun the approaching storm and get shelter that way – but make sure you have adequate fuel for the task ahead.

The strength of the crew also needs to be considered and a beat upwind may tax an already tired crew. Finally, is it better to ride out the storm rather than try to run for shelter? There will be no easy answers but all these factors need to be considered.

RUNNING FOR SHELTER

THE EARLIER YOU MAKE THE DECISION WHETHER OR NOT TO SEEK SHELTER, THE BETTER CHANCE YOU HAVE OF A SUCCESSFUL OUTCOME.

47 WEATHER TACTICS

In looking at the tactics you can employ in relation to the weather, the first thing to remember is that you can't change the weather. However, what you can control to a certain extent is where you are in relation to the weather systems. In earlier sections we have discussed timing in relation to the weather, and the direction in which you are travelling will affect the timing, allowing the weather to catch up more slowly or to get past more quickly.

When you encounter a passing frontal system that may contain severe weather, you have two main choices. If you head into the weather, you may experience some difficult conditions for a while, but you'll pass through the front and emerge into the better conditions on the other side. If you run downwind before the front, you're likely to get a more comfortable ride and delay the frontal conditions catching up with you.

To make tactical decisions like this, you need to have a good handle on the weather and its timing. Once you have this, your decision is likely to be influenced by what lies further along your chosen course. As discussed in Running for shelter, 46, if heading into the bad weather takes you closer to shelter, this may be the best option; or perhaps the wind will shift round to a point where it is now coming off the land and the fetch will be much shorter. On the other hand, the option of running downwind may buy you time to reach shelter of some sort and avoid the worst of the weather.

So much will depend on the local topography, on what the forecaster is predicting, on the location of your destination, even on the tides, because these can have a significant effect on sea conditions. The tactics are likely to be very different for sail and powerboats – under sail, you're restricted in the directions in which you can travel, while in a powerboat you have the benefit of speed and rapid progress, but your options may be limited by the amount of fuel on board.

There are so many options involved that the weather tactics you adopt are never going to be an easy decision. And just because you may be on a passage to a particular destination doesn't mean that you can't change that destination – this can be one of your strongest weapons in determining your weather tactics.

COASTAL TACTICS 48

Running under the shelter of the land may allow a passage to be completed when conditions further out at sea are untenable. However, do be aware of any forecast change to the wind direction, which might leave you exposed. Also remember that while the forecast may show the wind coming off the land, local winds will often run along the coastline rather than out from it because winds are channelled by high land.

Headlands are always a key point in any coastal passage and you have very few options if your passage plan includes rounding a headland. However, you can get considerable respite from the conditions when the wind is ahead if you head into the bays between the headlands rather than directly across (as long as there are no navigation dangers to impede your progress). The initial course of heading into the bay will put the wind off the bow, which for powerboats should give an easier ride. Then when you head along the coast on the inside of the bay you will come steadily into the more sheltered waters protected by the next headland. You should take this shelter right up to the headland, and even when rounding the headland you can often find better sea conditions close inshore where the tides are weaker.

For sailboats, which will be tacking into the headwind across the bay anyway, this could be a better option than heading out to sea on the tack that takes you to the next headland, although you could lose some of the wind strength in sheltered areas.

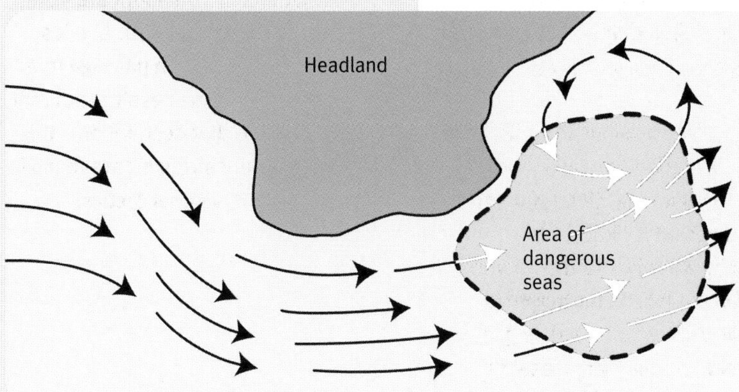

TIDAL CURRENT FLOW AROUND A PRONOUNCED HEADLAND.

49 WEATHER ROUTING

Weather routing is common practice for shipping but it is still in its infancy for small craft. Basically it means finding the optimum route on a passage that will allow you to take maximum advantage of the forecast weather conditions. You probably do a subconscious weather routing every time you go to sea, particularly in a sailboat where you want to get maximum advantage from the wind, and there is of course now the possibility of weather routing by computer.

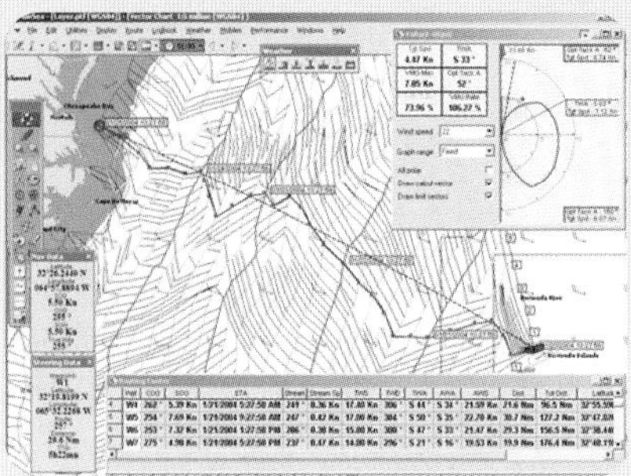

A WEATHER-ROUTING CHART FROM MAXSEA.

On a longer passage you may need to look ahead several days in your planning, and weather forecasts allow you to do that these days, although the accuracy of the forecast will inevitably deteriorate over time. Basic weather routing is simply a case of working out where you will be in, say, three days' time and seeing what the wind will be doing at that time and in that position.

You will want to set your course over the first couple of days to put yourself in the best position to take advantage of the weather conditions prevailing, but by looking ahead you can plan to be in the best position to take advantage of future weather.

Long-distance sailboat racers do this all the time, but weather routing can also be valuable for cruising yachts. Trying to work things out manually and look at all the options is not easy and there are now computer programmes that can do the sums for you. One of the specialist programmes is Maxsea, which first obtains an 8-day forecast by email and then works out from this the optimum sailing route to your destination. You will need to put into the computer a polar diagram of the performance of your yacht under different wind conditions, but once all the basic information is there it only takes the computer a few seconds to optimise the proposed route.

For power craft it is not so simple, because it is rare to find a polar diagram for these boats. Maxsea's programme for powerboats is due out this year, but it becomes more complex because there will be a much wider variety of speeds in different wind and sea conditions, and comfort levels on board also have to be considered. The programme for sailboats considers only the wind conditions that might be experienced and doesn't take into account the effect of the expected sea conditions – and it's the sea conditions that tend to affect the performance of powerboats, rather than the wind strengths and direction.

At present you have to do the weather routing for a powerboat manually, which you can do from experience. Powerboats tend to go on shorter passages than sailboats because of the need to refuel, but it could pay to tabulate the performance of the craft in different sea conditions and on different headings as the basis for a mental weather-routing exercise – remembering that the shortest route is not necessarily the quickest in a powerboat.

REMEMBER THAT THE SHORTEST ROUTE IS NOT NECESSARILY THE QUICKEST IN A POWERBOAT.

50 WEATHER LORE

When all else fails resort to old-fashioned weather lore! We all have weather sayings, most of which originated from childhood. Weather lore recalls the days when there were no weather forecasts as we know them today, and any forecast information was related to weather phenomena that could be observed, such as the clouds. These features enabled some sort of short-term forecasting to be made and, as this book highlights, this type of observation can help to put a timing on weather changes in your area. Some of these sayings may be stating the obvious, but they are still valid as an indication – although they offer no certainty.

- 'Red sky at night is the sailors' delight' and 'Red sky in the morning is the sailors' warning' are two of the best-known sayings, and these become valid when the weather is moving from west to east, as is normally the case. At night, the setting sun in the west will illuminate clouds that are moving off to the east, heralding the end of bad weather, while in the morning the rising sun will illuminate any clouds to the west, which herald possible worsening weather.

- 'Mackerel sky and mares' tails make lofty ships lower their sails' is a saying that relates to the high Cirrus clouds, followed by gradually lowering clouds, that are the first signs of an advancing warm front and worsening or changing weather.

- 'Rain before seven, fine by eleven' highlights the fact that the rain sector in an average warm front will not normally last more than four hours. The actual time of day has no bearing on the weather and the times could be any two figures – as long as they are four hours apart.

- 'First rise after a low foretells a stronger blow' is a description of what happens in some of the more active cold fronts. The heavier cold air coming in can cause a rapid increase in the pressure gradient, which is the first rise of the barometer after the low, and this is often associated with a considerable increase in the wind strength.

- 'When the wind backs and the barometer falls, then be on your guard against gales and squalls' is a pretty obvious reference to the situation of a falling barometer indicating the approach of bad weather. The 'wind backing' reference is what tends to happen with an advancing depression in the initial stages, provided that the centre is not too far north.

- Today, with sophisticated forecasting available at the touch of a button, these sayings have become more of a curiosity than a serious aid but when you have nothing else, they can still be very useful.

RED SKY AT NIGHT IS THE SAILORS' DELIGHT.

50 Ways to Improve Your Navigation
Dag Pike
ISBN 978-0-7136-8270-0

This book starts where most others finish. Packed with practical ways to make navigation safer, easier and better, the techniques cover sail and power as well as electronic and visual navigation.

50 Ways to Improve Your Navigation distils Dag Pike's experience gained from over 50 years of navigating a whole range of craft, and is your passport to practical navigation techniques that will get you safely to your destination whether in fine weather or foul.

50 Ways to Improve Your Powerboat Driving
Dag Pike
ISBN 978-0-7136-8269-4

This is a book about practical powerboat driving in boats large and small, and contains techniques that can only be picked up from experience – practical ways to make your driving safer, easier and better, whatever the conditions.

Dag Pike gives advice on handling a fast boat in waves and head seas, matching response times to sea conditions and using the throttle to affect trim. You may have learnt the important basics of powerboat driving, but now it's time to translate these into practical handling techniques to give a better ride and a smoother passage.